T0360451

Cultural Tourism and Cantonese Opera

Cultural tourism is an experiential tourism based on searching for and participating in new and deep cultural experiences. This book enhances the tourism literature by testing the tourist attitude towards related issues of Cantonese Opera as a cultural product of the Greater Bay Area.

This book starts with a general introduction to the background of Cantonese Opera. Chapter 2 is a historical review of Cantonese Opera development in the GBA. Chapter 3 introduces the concept of the Cantonese Opera as a cultural product. Chapter 4 discusses the related Cantonese Opera on tourism development in the GBA. Chapter 5 describes the trends of modernisation and integration of Cantonese Opera in the GBA. Lastly, Chapter 6 is a case study in Macau.

This book focuses on Cantonese Opera and cultural tourism. This means tourism practitioners and arts administrators should be the primary source of market and people in the rest of the world who are interested in Cantonese Opera and cultural tourism should find this book useful. This book is a valuable resource not only for social science researchers, but also for those in related fields, for example, arts administrators and tourism officers, among many others. This book could serve as a text for an advanced level undergraduate course for students in many of the arts administration and tourism fields. Additionally, this book is a valuable resource for teaching graduate students not only in tourism, but also in related fields. Furthermore, government or practitioners can improve the management of city and tourism service using this book.

Jian Ming Luo is an associate professor in Tourism Management, Macau, China.

Routledge Cultural Heritage and Tourism Series
Series editor: Dallen J. Timothy
Arizona State University, USA

The Routledge Cultural Heritage and Tourism Series offers an interdisciplinary social science forum for original, innovative and cutting-edge research about all aspects of cultural heritage-based tourism. This series encourages new and theoretical perspectives and showcases ground-breaking work that reflects the dynamism and vibrancy of heritage, tourism and cultural studies. It aims to foster discussions about both tangible and intangible heritages, and all of their management, conservation, interpretation, political, conflict, consumption and identity challenges, opportunities and implications. This series interprets heritage broadly and caters to the needs of upper-level students, academic researchers, and policy makers.

Resilience, Authenticity and Digital Heritage Tourism
Deepak Chhabra

Cultural Heritage and Tourism in Japan
Takamitsu Jimura

Medieval Imaginaries in Tourism, Heritage and the Media
Jennifer Frost and Warwick Frost

Children, Young People and Dark Tourism
Edited by Mary Margaret Kerr, Philip Stone and Rebecca H. Price

Tourism and Development in the Himalaya
Social, Environmental and Economic Forces
Edited by Gyan Nyaupane and Dallen J. Timothy

Cultural Tourism and Cantonese Opera
Jian Ming Luo

For more information about this series, please visit: www.routledge.com/
Routledge-Cultural-Heritage-and-Tourism-Series/book-series/RCHT

Cultural Tourism and Cantonese Opera

Jian Ming Luo

Routledge
Taylor & Francis Group

LONDON AND NEW YORK

First published 2022
by Routledge
4 Park Square, Milton Park, Abingdon, Oxon OX14 4RN

and by Routledge
605 Third Avenue, New York, NY 10158

Routledge is an imprint of the Taylor & Francis Group, an informa business

© 2022 Jian Ming Luo

The right of Jian Ming Luo to be identified as author of this work has been asserted in accordance with sections 77 and 78 of the Copyright, Designs and Patents Act 1988.

All rights reserved. No part of this book may be reprinted or reproduced or utilised in any form or by any electronic, mechanical, or other means, now known or hereafter invented, including photocopying and recording, or in any information storage or retrieval system, without permission in writing from the publishers.

Trademark notice: Product or corporate names may be trademarks or registered trademarks, and are used only for identification and explanation without intent to infringe.

British Library Cataloguing-in-Publication Data
A catalogue record for this book is available from the British Library

Library of Congress Cataloging-in-Publication Data
A catalog record for this book has been requested

ISBN: 978-0-367-74381-9 (hbk)
ISBN: 978-0-367-74382-6 (pbk)
ISBN: 978-1-003-15756-4 (ebk)

DOI: 10.4324/9781003157564

Typeset in Times New Roman
by Apex CoVantage, LLC

Contents

Figures

Tables

Preface

The Guangdong-Hong Kong-Macao Greater Bay Area (GBA) comprises Hong Kong, Macau and nine municipalities in Guangdong, China. The nine municipalities are Guangzhou, Shenzhen, Zhuhai, Foshan, Huizhou, Dongguan, Zhongshan, Jiangmen and Zhaoqing. The key focus of the GBA is to enhance, extend and deepen cooperation between Guangdong, Hong Kong, and Macau by leveraging the comparative advantage of all cities in the GBA. On 1 July 2017, witnessed by President Xi Jinping, the National Development and Reform Commission and the governments of Guangdong, Hong Kong and Macao signed the Framework Agreement on Deepening Guangdong-Hong Kong-Macao Cooperation in the Development of the GBA. Macau government liberalised its gambling industry in 2002. Since then, the top priority of the government (both Macau and China) was to diversify the gambling industry. Since Macau is one of the core cities in the GBA, it takes forward its development as a global tourism and leisure centre, establishes an economic and trade cooperation platform between China and Portuguese-speaking countries and fosters the appropriately diversified and sustainable development of the economy in Macau. Since Cantonese Opera is one of the major representatives of the Lingnan Culture, which are represented by Cantonese Opera, Dragon Boat, Lion Dance, and Martial Arts, it should play a role in the promotion of the Lingnan Culture.

Cultural tourism is an experiential tourism based on searching for and participating in new and deep cultural experiences. A cultural tourist seeks a variety of cultural experiences such as aesthetic, intellectual, emotional or psychological. Cultural tourism is a tool to enhance the economic efficiency and destination image of the Greater Bay Area. Hence, it is important to develop cultural tourism sustainably such that the attractiveness of the tourism products can be preserved. Recently, local governments have attempted to promote the attitude of both domestic and international tourists via different channels. These promotions attract many tourists to travel to the local area. The results of this study can provide suggestions and recommendations to the planning and design of the cultural and leisure products, improve the brand of the tourism products, and eventually develop cultural tourism sustainably. This type of study is relatively new in the tourism and hospitality literature. Particularly, this issue seldom appeared in tourism and hospitality literature. Therefore, this book enhances tourism literature by testing the tourist attitude towards related issues of Cantonese Opera as a cultural product of the Greater Bay Area. Furthermore, government or practitioners can improve the management of city and tourism service using this book.

Chapter 1 is a general introduction to the Cantonese Opera in China and around the world. Chapter 2 is a historical review of Cantonese Opera development in Guangdong, Hong Kong and Macau. Chapter 3 discusses the concept of Cantonese Opera as a cultural product. Chapter 4 focuses on the development of cultural tourism in the GBA. Chapter 5 describes the trends of modernisation and integration of Cantonese Opera in the GBA. Chapter 6 investigates residents' attitudes towards Cantonese Opera as a tourism product in Macau. A qualitative approach is designed and analysed using content analysis. This case study will provide theoretical and practical perspective on Cantonese Opera's influence on tourism development in the Greater Bay Area.

Acknowledgements

This book owes so much debt to many people and organisations, especially their comments and support. Their comments are extremely valuable to this book. The Faculty of International Tourism and Management at the City University of Macau provided an excellent research environment to complete and develop this book. The Macau Foundation also provided the funding of some of the research of this book.

Many of my friends and colleagues helped me with this book. However, I would like to thank Professor Rob Law, Professor Kuai Peng Ip, Professor Hanqin Qiu, Professor Ivan Lai, Professor Xi Li, Dr. Hong Chen, Dr. Iok Teng Kou, Dr. Jian Yang, and Dr. Yulan Fan, in particular. In addition, my graduate students, Ziye Shang, Yu Pan, Liang Liu, Yingzhi Li, Li Zhou, and Xiang Zheng have put tremendous effort into conducting the research. Their help and contributions in maintaining the quality of this book are greatly appreciated. Without all of your support, this book would not be able to be accomplished.

Last, but by no means least, I would like to thank my family and partner for their encouragement and support. Justin Luo made a big difference – not least all the hours of fun and enjoyment. Without them, I would not have been able to complete this book.

Jian Ming Luo
Macau, China
March, 2022

1 An Introduction to Cantonese Opera

1.1 Background of Cantonese Opera

1.1.1 Cantonese Opera: Cantonese Performing Art

Cantonese opera is a traditional Chinese art form that transforms music, singing, martial arts, acrobatics and acting into a performance with rich symbolic meaning (Zhang, 2007). However, the language for delivering the performance is Cantonese, as the name suggests. The story in the opera usually involves history, traditions, culture and philosophies. The origin of Cantonese opera can be traced back 300 years. The influence of Cantonese opera in Southern China is massive. It is considered the Masterpiece of the Oral and Intangible Heritage of Humanity by UNESCO in 2009 (Macao Government Tourism Office, 2021). The primary language used in Macau is Cantonese. Thus, Cantonese opera is also popular in Macau. The total number of troupes in Macau is 260 (CNTV, 2014).

Chinese opera or *xiqu* comprises more than 350 kinds (Leung, 2017). Cantonese opera, a type of Chinese opera, is defined as 'story-telling through singing and dancing' (Tai, 2020). It tells a story using different instruments, dancing techniques and music (Tai, 2020). Cantonese opera is also known as Guangdong Drama because it is mainly performed and found in the Guangdong area. However, it is also extremely popular in Hong Kong, Macau, Malaysia and Singapore. The stories in Cantonese operas are usually based on historical figures and legends. These stories deliver not only Chinese culture and philosophy, such as loyalty, faith and patriotism (Wertz, 2016), but also distinct characteristics of the Lingnan (Cantonese) culture. The music, as well as the lyrics, demonstrates the expressiveness and beauty of Cantonese opera. The martial art performance is performed as a form of fighting arts (The Academy of Chinese Studies, 2020) (see Figure 1.1).

DOI: 10.4324/9781003157564-1

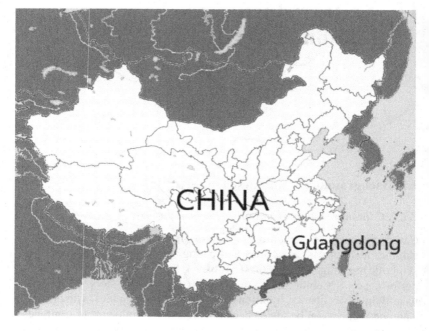

Figure 1.1 Map of Guangdong Province

1.1.2 *Origin of Cantonese Opera*

Various speculations on the origins of Cantonese opera exist. Duhalde et al. (2019) suggested that the origin of Cantonese opera can be traced back to the reign of Emperor Ming-Huang Tang (713–756 AD). However, Tai (2020) suggested that Cantonese opera started during the reign of Emperor Qian-long (1735–1796 AD). The research team at the City University of Hong Kong argued that Cantonese opera originated in the Ming dynasty (The City University of Hong Kong, 2020). Ng (2015) provided a detailed description of the development of Cantonese opera from a historical perspective. According to Ng (2015), Cantonese opera evolved from Zaju (a poetic music drama) and Chuanqi (a short legend telling act). Both acts are active in the Song (960–1279) and Yuan (1279–1368) dynasties. After the Yuan dynasty was taken over by the Ming dynasty (1368–1644), theatres become popular. The following are the three main branches that developed in this period: Yiyang developed in Jiangxi; Bangzi developed in Shanxi, Shenxi and Hebei; and Kunqu developed in Jiangnan. All branches are very popular in China. However, Cantonese opera does not begin in Guangdong. According to Song (1994) and Zhong (2014), Cantonese opera became popular in Shanghai in the 1840s. Many Guangdong businessmen travel to Shanghai for business purposes. However, as they became influential in Shanghai, they began to sponsor some cultural activities, including Cantonese opera. They started with small sponsor activities, but later, they also opened Cantonese opera companies. Many businessmen invite their friends, relatives or business partners to enjoy Cantonese opera. The development of Cantonese opera in Shanghai was highly successful in the 1920s to 1930s (Song, 1994; Zhong, 2014; Cheng, 2007).

Despite the academic debate of the origin of Cantonese opera, the influence of Cantonese opera is massive. During the Qing dynasty, particularly under Emperor Qianlong (1736–1795), many Cantonese troupes were in Foshan. However, the Qing government decided to ban Cantonese opera because of a political movement led by a Cantonese opera artist during the Taiping Rebellion. Many Cantonese opera troupes were renamed or repackaged as *Peking Opera troupes* to continue their performance. Later, when the ban was lifted, many troupes moved their base from Foshan to Guangzhou. An artist association named Pak Wo Association (or Chinese Artistic Association) was formed in 1889. Cantonese opera began to spread to Guangxi, and the primary language used to deliver the act gradually changed to Cantonese instead of Mandarin (Hong Kong Memory, 2020).

Cantonese opera is an important icon for the Cantonese (Lingnan) culture. Many famous Cantonese operas were filmed as movies in the 1940s. Cantonese opera is an essential element in Cantonese culture. Nearly all Cantonese people have heard Cantonese operas somehow, such as Tang Disheng's *Princess Chang Ping* and *Legends of Purple Hairpin*. The later Cantonese dramas and Cantonese songs are said to develop from Cantonese opera. Cantonese opera is a very representative traditional culture of highly native characteristics in Cantonese culture. Recently, many Hong Kong movies have been based on stories related to Cantonese opera. Here are a few examples:

Hu Du Men

Hu Du Men was produced by Golden Harvest Entertainment in 1996. *Hu Du Men* refers to an imaginary 'door' dividing the stage and the real world. According to the movie, actors or actresses should completely forget about themselves and become the characters they perform once they have passed this door. The story is about how a famous Cantonese opera actress (who pretends to be male in the opera character) has performed on stage for more than 30 years. She struggles between family, love, kids and her career.

The film also discusses the challenges and difficulties of the modernisation of Cantonese opera.

The Mad Phoenix

The Mad Phoenix was also produced in 1996. The main character, Jiang Yu Liu, is a legendary Cantonese opera script writer in the 1930s. The movie shows the development of Cantonese opera during the same period in Hong Kong and Guangzhou. Jiang Yu Liu enjoys opera very much. He skips school to go watch opera every day. He is exceptionally talented in script writing and produces many famous Cantonese opera plays (The City University of Hong Kong, 2020)

Despite being a prevalent form of entertainment, Cantonese opera often carries certain messages or lessons. This feature was vital before formal education was common across the country (Wertz, 2016). The government sometimes uses this platform to deliver the idea of 'being loyal to the emperor and love the kingdom'. Hence, opera scripts, which are highly scrutinised, may be banned if the government does not approve the message delivered (Wertz, 2016). In addition, Cantonese opera reflects society and is closely related to people's identity (Chung, 2017). In the 20th century, many troupes mainly performed in Guangzhou, Hong Kong and Macau, whilst others mainly performed in the rural areas in mainland China. The former is called *Sheng Gang daban*, whereas the latter is called *Guo Shan ban* (Zhuhai College of Jilin University, 2020). During the civil wars in China of 1927–1949, many people fled from Guangdong to Hong Kong to seek a stable and comfortable life. This movement provided opportunities for the development of Cantonese opera in Hong Kong. During that period, Hong Kong was a British colony. Troupes in Hong Kong were allowed to be exposed to many Western cultures and presentation methods. This situation was crucial to the development of Cantonese opera (Chung, 2017; Zhuhai College of Jilin University, 2020). Many new plays, such as *The Purple Hairpin* and *Di Nu Hua*, were written during this period (Zhuhai College of Jilin University, 2020). At the same time, many influential actors, actresses or troupes were discovered. Yam Kim Fai, Pak Suet Sin, Fong Yim Fun and Leung Sin Poh are the representative actors and actresses (Tai, 2020). Yam Kam Fai and Pak Suet Sin developed Sin Fung Ming Opera Troupe and Chor Fung Ming Opera Troupe, which are the most influential troupes in the history of Cantonese opera in Hong Kong (Zhuhai College of Jilin University, 2020). Xue Juexian, Sun Ma Sze Tsang and Hung Sin Nui developed Chun Sin Mei Opera Troupe, aiming at reviving Cantonese opera. This period is the golden age of Cantonese opera in Hong Kong (Education University in Hong Kong, 2015) (see Figure 1.2).

Figure 1.2 Cantonese Opera in Hong Kong

1.1.3 Current status of Cantonese Opera

Cantonese opera was very popular in the 19th century. However, on the one hand, people's enthusiasm for Cantonese opera diminished as other forms of entertainment, such as movies, music and video games, emerged. On the other hand, the number of audiences declined because many young people do not have the interest and the knowledge to appreciate Cantonese opera (Leung, 2017; Mei et al., 2018). Moreover, the lack of interest from younger generations leads to a drop in new participants. Many plays and scripts are relatively old, and no new play or script is written. *Princess Chang Ping*, *Flirting Scholar* and *Parted Lovers* are certainly famous plays to the older generations, but they lack attraction to the younger generation. Some of the classic plays have been reproduced several times throughout history. In addition, when an existing play is reproduced, people compare the new version with the old. If the latest version does not meet the expectation of the audiences, particularly when the old version is legendary, then even the existing viewers gradually lose interest. This scenario also causes the industrial producers' lack of interest to create (Mei et al., 2018). Hence, the number of Cantonese opera performances in bamboo shed theatres in Hong Kong dwindled from 158 in 1970 to 34 in 2010. The traditional bamboo sheds where operas are performed and the accompanying communal rituals are also under threat (The University of Hong Kong Knowledge Exchange, 2020).

Numerous actions have been taken to restore or preserve this significant and influential art form. Since Hong Kong was returned to China in 1997, the Education Bureau in Hong Kong has been updating the education system of primary and secondary schools. Chinese music has been recently included in the Hong Kong Diploma of Secondary Education, and opera is a part of the listening paper. Teachers are encouraged to use Cantonese opera as a platform to teach Chinese music. Furthermore, the Hong Kong Academy for Performing Arts (HKAPA) introduced a 4-year Bachelor of Fine Arts programme with a degree in Chinese opera (Cantonese Opera Performance or Cantonese Opera Music) to provide formal education of Chinese Arts instead of relying on traditional teacher – apprentice teaching methods (HKAPA, 2020; Leung, 2017). In China, the protection of the Cantonese opera began with the proposal initiated by a National People's Congress member in Guangdong. Seminars were held to collect opinions and comments on how to preserve the culture of Cantonese opera legally. A formal Cantonese opera teaching system, like the one offered by the HKAPA, was introduced in 2014. At the same time, a database regarding Cantonese opera was developed to document and record the history and development of Cantonese opera properly. Various forms of legislation were approved by the government to provide legal protection and inheritance of Cantonese opera (Mei et al., 2018).

Traditional Cantonese opera troupes also try to adapt to the new environment to overcome the lack of audience. On the one hand, they try to create new plays and expand the audience from mainly Chinese to Western people. Initiated by Wah Yan Dramatic Society, Cantonese opera performing in English began in 1947. Sunbeam Theatre and famous Cantonese opera screenwriter Li Kui Ming have recently produced a Cantonese opera called *Trump on Show*. The story is about Donald Trump and China; in this opera, up-to-date materials are attempted to be incorporated into Cantonese opera in Hong Kong (Ramzy, 2019). In 2017, Zeng Xiaomin, together with many other actors, performed *Madame White Snake – The Affection*, which is a spin of the classic *Madame White Snake*. The new show incorporates new fashion and technologies, such as LED screens with animations and modern stage design, to the classic play. Many people, including artists in China, praise the performance of Zeng Xiaomin. They claim that Zeng's performance demonstrates professional excellence and continuous improvement over her career (Prnewswire, 2017).

1.2 Importance of Cantonese Opera

1.2.1 Cantonese (Lingnan) Culture in China

Lingnan is located on the southern edge of the East Asia continent. It also connects to Southeast Asia, Oceania and Central and East Africa. It is also the starting point of the Silk Road on the sea in ancient times. Historically, Guangzhou is a popular hub for foreign people to enter China. Moreover, many people in Lingnan immigrate to other countries. Approximately 30 million Chinese people are living outside China, and more than two-thirds of them are Cantonese. The unique geographic and population advantage allows Lingnan to become a very open, diverse and accepting environment. Ever since the Han dynasty, Lingnan has been importing many foreign products. These products exhibit not only economic values but also cultural meanings. For example, many religious beliefs, such as Islam, Buddhism and Christianity, as well as much Western knowledge and science, are imported. This knowledge eventually spills over to other parts of China. The important consequence of this is that the Lingnan people improve themselves during interaction with the West. Lingnan people learn their weaknesses and try to improve themselves. This change becomes apparent after the Opium War. Many philosophers, politicians and revolutionists introduce Western philosophies and political standpoints. Hence, Lingnan becomes one of the testing points for many opening policies and eventually establishes many remarkable achievements. Guangzhou is the centre, model and representative of Lingnan culture. It is also the political, economic and social centre of South China. The influence of Guangzhou has already exceeded its geographical position. Other places such as Hakka, Chaoshan and the Pearl River Delta are influenced by Guangzhou culture (Huang, 2019). Guangzhou is a city with rich and abundant history and culture. It is one of the national historical and cultural cities promulgated by the

State Council (Liu, 2016). It also becomes one of the role models for many cities in the world. The rich historical content, as well as classic modern culture, makes Lingnan one of the most attractive destinations to many local and foreign visitors (Liu, 2016).

1.2.2 Cantonese Opera in Lingnan Culture

Cantonese opera is an important part of Lingnan culture. Cantonese opera, Guangdong music and Nanling painting are known as the *Lingnan Three Shows* (Zhang, 2018). Guangzhou is the centre of Lingnan culture. In Guangzhou, you can find Lingnan calligraphy, Lingnan painting school, Lingnan poetry, Lingnan architecture, Lingnan bonsai, Lingnan craft to Lingnan folk and Lingnan food culture. From the Temple of the Six Banyan Trees and Nanhai Guanyin Temple to Dr. Sun Yat-sen Memorial Hall and Chen Clan Ancestral Hall, one can appreciate how architecture has changed over the years. Qing Hui Yuan allows people to enjoy not only a bit of the natural beauty in Guangzhou but also the great rich history embedded in the architecture. The Sacred Heart Cathedral witnessed the importance of Guangzhou as a hub to connect China and the world. The Cantonese Opera Tea House allows people to enjoy Cantonese opera whilst having a nice cup of Chinese tea (Mei et al., 2018). Lingnan culture is an integral part of splendid Chinese culture. It is not only a native culture which possesses many traditional characteristics of other Chinese cultures but also an integrated culture which adopts many foreign cultures. Hence, Lingnan culture also contains many qualities of other cultures, such as pragmatism, openness and diversity (Guangzhou International, 2020). Starting from 1987, Guangzhou has been holding the Guangzhou Folk Art Festival. This festival increases the number of visitors in Guangzhou. This folk art festival is a tremendous success. This event shows that Guangzhou is a unique city with charming and attractive cultural resources which shed light on the development of tourism in Guangzhou (Liu, 2016). Cantonese opera is popular with Cantonese people all over the world. As an important part of Cantonese culture, Cantonese opera can stimulate audiences' cultural memory and cultural identity. This kind of cultural identity strengthens the emotional connection between Cantonese opera audiences and Cantonese opera, allowing them to consume and appreciate this kind of performing arts and affecting their consumption experience of Cantonese opera (Yang et al., 2021).

1.3 Profile of the Cantonese Opera in the World

Cantonese opera is the song for everyone in all the Chinatowns in the world. Whenever Cantonese opera music starts, people in Chinatown are immersed in the joyful atmosphere and memorable moments. Many Chinese have immigrated to Los Angeles, San Francisco, New York and Boston in the last few decades. Hence, a Chinatown in each corresponding city has emerged. People in Chinatown enrich the cultural and entertainment activities of the Chinese community, promote Chinese culture and carry out many voluntary works (Huang, 2019). Many Chinese immigrated to the Pacific Rim in the late 19th century. They showed a considerable amount of interest in Cantonese opera, which created a huge opportunity for troupes in mainland China to play in areas such as Singapore, Indonesia, San Francisco and New York (Ng, 2015). At the beginning of the 20th century, many overseas actors and actresses have promoted democracy and revolution via Cantonese opera. Many troupes began to rely heavily on overseas performance income. According to Zhong (2015), more than 8 million Chinese live overseas, and approximately 70% are Cantonese. These Chinese are mainly living in Asia and America. As Cantonese opera became increasingly popular overseas, many Cantonese opera theatres and companies emerged. These theatres and companies provide additional performing opportunities for many local troupes as the competition in Hong Kong and Guangzhou intensifies. Some actors or actresses use their overseas performance to boost their popularity domestically (Ng, 2015).

The contribution of the Bahe Huiguan (Pak Wo Association) should not be neglected. Cantonese opera has existed in China for more than 400 years. Given the popularity of Cantonese opera in China, some actors and actresses have established Qionghua Huiguan to act as a communication hub for troupes, screenwriters, actors and actresses. It was the first industrial community of Cantonese opera. However, several actors and actresses from Qionghua Huiguan joined the Taiping Rebellion. Thus, the Qing dynasty destroyed Qionghua Huiguan and banned the performance of Cantonese opera as a punishment. Cantonese opera could not perform until 1875, when those actors and actresses who joined the Taiping Rebellion passed away. The Qing dynasty relaxed the punishment and eventually allowed Cantonese opera performance. Some actors and actresses re-established a communication hub called Bahe Huiguan. Ever since its establishment, many Bahe Huiguan have been established in the world. In 1953, the Bahe Huiguan in Hong Kong officially registered its name as the Chinese Artists Association of Hong Kong (The Chinese Artists Association of Hong Kong, 2020). At present, many Bahe Huiguan are established in the world, including Holland, UK, Switzerland, Germany, Belgium, Malaysia, San Francisco, New York, Macau, Hong Kong and Guangdong. According to Wang (2020b), the purpose of Pak Wo Association nowadays involves (1) saving the traditional skills, which includes systematic research and data collection of Cantonese opera, and establishing an open database of Cantonese opera;

(2) providing professional training, which includes the incorporation of modern management methods, enhancing management structure and increasing the opportunities of practice; (3) expanding markets, which includes the development and cultivation of Cantonese opera market, conducting systematic marketing research and increasing promotion; (4) standing on the shoulders of giants, which means creating, practising and developing Cantonese opera with a spirit of preserving the traditions.

1.3.1 Cantonese Opera in Singapore

As the overseas market developed, Singapore and San Francisco, two places where many Chinese people resided, were eventually developed into two major hubs of Cantonese opera (Ng, 2015). Since the opening of Singapore in 1819, many Cantonese troupes had travelled to Singapore to perform as many labourers came to this country to work. On some festivals or birthdays of a Chinese god, such as Buddha, some businesses or associations would invite Cantonese opera troupes to perform. Many Chinese immigrants watched Cantonese opera together. These performances were usually free. As the number of Cantonese immigrants increased considerably during the 1920s, Cantonese opera became increasingly popular in the community (Chong, 2003). Pear Garden (or the later Chinese Artistic Association in Singapore) was formed. Many actors and actresses moved to Singapore after the Taiping Rebellion. Given that the Singapore government required every social group to register, Pear Garden was registered as Bahe Huiguan in Singapore.

As Cantonese opera began to spread worldwide, many Bahe Huiguan (or the Chinese Artistic Association) were established (Liu, 2016). In the last century, Bahe Huiguan not only nurtured many talented actors and actresses but also performed in many places in the world. For example, Bahe Huiguan in Singapore visited Hong Kong to perform for The Community Chest in 1973, and the association also visited Germany to perform at the Projekt Berlin in 1978. In 1996, the association performed *Forty Years of Cherished Love* at the International Cantonese Opera Festival (Wang, 2020a). Despite performing on stage, the association often serves in the community, such as schools, to increase people's interest in Cantonese opera, especially that of the younger generations.

This development, including the resurgence of performances by troupes from China and the revival of local amateur troupes, is part of the efforts by the government and various community associations to preserve and promote Cantonese opera as part of Singapore's cultural heritage. *Professional* and *amateur* are terms used in Singapore to differentiate between types of performers. Professional troupes perform for profit, whereas amateur troupes do so for leisure and interest. The terms are not indicative of the skills and standards of the performers. Professional troupes, supported mainly by Chinese religious institutions, still perform during religious festivals and ceremonies. Amateur troupes put up performances in highly publicised government-sponsored events, like the Hong Lim Park Chinese Opera series staged annually at the park between 1978 and 1985 and the Singapore Street Opera Festival held in 2004 in the central business, shopping and tourist districts.

1.3.2 Cantonese Opera in North America

With its elaborate costumes, lively music, engaging stories and powerful vocal delivery, Cantonese opera is one of the many forms of traditional Chinese theatre which captivates audiences around the world. In Canada, this genre is particularly significant within Chinese – Canadian communities. More than one million Cantonese are living in Canada. Most of them are in Vancouver and Toronto, which are also important centres for Cantonese opera in Canada. Some Cantonese opera troupes also perform in Victoria, Calgary, Edmonton, Winnipeg and Montreal.

The history of Chinese immigrants to Canada can be dated back to 150 years ago. People came to Canada and worked in the mine in the Fraser Valley or on the Canadian Pacific Railway in British Columbia. From 1881 to 1885, more than 17,000 Chinese moved to Canada, and this number reached 40,000 in 1921.

Cantonese opera has long been an important cultural touchstone for Chinese Canadians. Three Cantonese opera theatres were established in British Columbia in the 1880s. Many Cantonese opera troupes performed not only in Canada but also in Hong Kong and China during those times. Thus, Cantonese opera also served as a connector of cultural heritage between these areas. In the 1920s, many local associations were developed in Canada to rehearse and study Chinese operatic traditions (Rao, 2014). Given that an increasing number of Chinese immigrants were moving to Canada, Cantonese opera was also an important method to raise funds for many social and political events. Many of these associations continue to exist today, and they continue to contribute to the Cantonese opera community by teaching Cantonese opera to the younger generation, enhancing the artistic level and promoting Cantonese opera to Western society.

Cantonese opera also gained much popularity because of the development of commercial recordings. In 1904, many international recording companies began to distribute Cantonese opera records in North America. Amongst these recording companies, Montreal's Berliner Gram-o-phone Co. Limited, later known as the Victor Talking Machine Company of Canada, was considered the most active recording company.

As the number of Chinese people from Hong Kong and mainland China immigrating to the United States increased in the last few decades, not only the population of Chinese in the United States increased, but also the popularity of Chinatown in each area intensified. The operation of Cantonese opera in these areas returned to normal. According to Huang (2019), more than 70 Cantonese opera associations or communities can be found in the United States, for example, Nanzhongguo Yueshe in San Francisco and Guangdong Music Research Society in Boston. These communities provided enormous enjoyment and fun to the Chinese people in the United States (Huang, 2019).

The first Cantonese troupe that appeared in the United States is Hong Fook Tang in 1852. The troupe first arrived in San Francisco, probably because of the large Chinese population at that time. They continued their performance in New York and Washington. Once the performance became a success, other troupes in China followed. The first Cantonese opera theatre was established in 1867, and many followed. The establishment of the Cantonese opera theatre in Victoria is not without reason. In the late 19th century, the Gold Rush in the Fraser Canyon attracted many Chinese. Furthermore, Sir John A. Macdonald employed many Chinese workers to build the Canadian Pacific Railway, thereby encouraging many Chinese to arrive. In addition, the anti-Chinese campaign in San Francisco began to arise, pushing the Chinese population and the theatres to other places in the United States and Canada (Ng, 2015).

The development of Cantonese opera in North America came with setbacks. For example, the federal government of Canada passed the Chinese Immigration Act in the early 1900s. The Act imposed a heavy head tax on each Chinese immigrant (Rao, 2014). This event, as well as the anti-Chinese campaign in San Francisco mentioned in the previous paragraph, reduced Chinese people's incentive to immigrate, reducing the population and audience. Moreover, many North Americans did not really appreciate the beauty of Cantonese opera. An anonymous writer in *Harper's Weekly* said Cantonese Opera 'has no dignity, no repose, [and] no beauty' and the play is 'childish'. Another writer from *Cosmopolitan* also said Cantonese opera actors waste too much time to sing, and the script is poorly written (Ng, 2015). As one can easily predict, the number of troupes performing in North America reduced dramatically. The situation did not improve after the new China (The People's Republic of China) was established. In 1952, the Great China Theatre in San Francisco recruited several famous Cantonese actors and actresses to form the first of what we have now known as residency shows in San Francisco. Thus, many troupes that reside in the United States began to perform regularly. As the US – China relationship began to improve, other troupes in China performed regularly in the United States.

Together with the troupes residing in the United States, they attracted many people interested in Cantonese opera to promote and teach Cantonese opera in the United States (Yao, 2020).

1.4 Summary

Cantonese opera is a part of Chinese opera. Its origins can be traced back to the Qing dynasty. Foshan, a city of Guangdong, is usually considered the centre of Cantonese opera. Some Cantonese opera performers joined the Taipei rebellion. Thus, the Qing government banned Cantonese opera until the Tongzhi period. During this period, the centre of Cantonese opera gradually shifted to Guangzhou. After the ban was lifted, Cantonese opera gradually spread this traditional Chinese art form to the rest of the world with the development of the Chinese Artists Association. In 2009, Cantonese opera was incorporated in the UNESCO Representative List of Intangible Cultural Heritage.

References

The Academy of Chinese Studies. (2020). *The Splendid Chinese Culture*. Retrieved October 13, 2020, from https://en.chiculture.net/?file=topic_details&old_id=30011.

Cheng, M. P. (2007). The Trans-locality of Local Cultures in Modern China: Cantonese Opera, Music, and Songs in Shanghai, 1920s–1930s. *Modern Chinese History Studies*, 2007(2), 1–17.

The Chinese Artist Association of Hong Kong. (2020). *Introduction*. Retrieved December 26, 2020, from www.hkbarwo.com/aboutus_aim.php.

The City University of Hong Kong. (2020). *The Origins of Cantonese Opera*. Retrieved October 13, 2020, from www.cityu.edu.hk/lib/about/event/cantonese_opera/origins.htm.

Chong, T. (2003). Chinese Opera in Singapore: Negotiating Globalisation, Consumerism and National Culture. *Journal of Southeast Asian Studies*, 449–471.

Chung, N. (2017). *Fading or Flourishing? Cantonese Opera in Hong Kong*. Retrieved October 21, 2020, from https://medium.com/@nicole.c/fading-or-flourishing-cantonese-opera-in-hong-kong-b1e93d6150b6.

CNTV. (2014). *Macao Cantonese Opera Thrives with Portuguese Folk Dances*. Retrieved March 1, 2020, from http://english.www.gov.cn/news/video/2014/12/19/content_281475026518336.htm.

Duhalde, M., Yan, J. T., & Wong, D. (2019, November 8). *Cantonese Performing Art*. Retrieved October 13, 2020, from https://multimedia.scmp.com/infographics/culture/article/3036661/cantonese-opera/index.html.

Education University in Hong Kong. (2015). *Cantonese Opera in Hong Kong*. Retrieved October 21, 2020, from www.ied.edu.hk/ccaproject/yueju/eng/index_hk.php.

Guangzhou International. (2020). *Culture and History*. Retrieved November 4, 2020, from www.gz.gov.cn/guangzhouinternational/visitors/whattosee/cultureandhistory/content/post_3012710.html.

Hong Kong Academy of Performing Arts (HKAPA). (2020). *Bachelor of Fine Arts (Honours) Degree in Chinese Opera.* Retrieved December 31, 2020, from www. hkapa.edu/co/study-programmes/bachelor-of-fine-arts-honours-degree-in-chinese-opera.

Hong Kong Memory. (2020). *The Origin of Cantonese Opera.* Retrieved October 13, 2020, from www.hkmemory.hk/MHK/collections/ichhk/opera/origin/index.html.

Huang, M. (2019, May). Research on the Innovation and Shaping of Urban Culture Brand Image from the Perspective of Regional Economy – Taking Guangzhou as an Example. *IOP Conference Series: Earth and Environmental Science,* 267(5), 052042. IOP Publishing.

Leung, B. W. (2017). *Transmission of Cantonese Opera in Hong Kong: Issues and Challenges.* Retrieved October 25, 2020, from https://theasiadialogue.com/2017/07/26/transmission-of-cantonese-opera-in-hong-kong-issues-and-challenges/.

Liu, Y. (2016). Devekionebt of the Cultural Tourism Resources in GuangDong. *Tropical Geography,* 16(3), 276–282.

Macao Government Tourism Office. (2021). *Shows.* Retrieved March 1, 2021, from www.macaotourism.gov.mo/en/shows-and-entertainment/shows/yueju-opera-cantonese-opera.

Mei, Y., Guo, M., Lin, M., Jiang, G., Zhou, J., Zhou, H., . . . Xie, M. (2018, December). Protection and Inheritance of Cantonese Opera. In *2nd International Conference on Art Studies: Science, Experience, Education (ICASSEE 2018).* Dordrecht, The Netherlands: Atlantis Press.

Ng, W. C. (2015). *The Rise of Cantonese Opera.* Champaign, IL , USA: University of Illinois Press.

PR Newswire. (2017). Zeng Xiaomin, a Leading Diva of Contemporary Cantonese Opera. Retrieved March 2, 2021, from www.prnewswire.com/news-releases/zeng-xiaomin-a-leading-diva-of-contemporary-cantonese-opera-300569951.html.

Ramzy, A. (2019, May 08). *A Trump Bump for Hong Kong's Last Commercial Cantonese Opera Theater.* Retrieved from www.nytimes.com/2019/05/08/world/asia/trump-opera-hong-kong.html.

Rao, N. (2014). Chinese Opera in Turn-of-the Century Canada: Local History and Transnational Circulation. *Nineteenth-Century Music Review,* 11(2), 291–310. doi:10.1017/S1479409814000391.

Song, Z. Y. 宋钻友 (1994). 粤剧在旧上海的演出. *Shinlin*史林 (1), 64–70.

Tai, S. Y. (2020). *Introduction to Cantonese Opera.* Hong Kong Education City, Hong Kong Education City Limited. Retrieved October 21, 2020, from www.hkedcity. net/res_data/edbltr-ae/1-1000/a11ad5dd9fa0d7bdd20b5c973422de0791/intro-duction_to_cantonese_opera_eng_upload_150825.pdf.

The University of Hong Kong Knowledge Exchange. (2020). *Breathing New Life into Art form at Risk: Cantonese Opera.* Retrieved October 25, 2020, from www. ke.hku.hk/story/all/breathing-new-life-into-an-art-form-at-risk-cantonese-opera.

Wang, H. N. (2020a). 浅谈粤剧在新加坡的发展. Retrieved December 26, 2020, from www.foshanmuseum.com/learning/detail.html?id=9482.

Wang, L. (2020b). *The Chinese Artist Association of Hong Kong.* Retrieved December 26, 2020, from www.lizawang.com/talk/talk142_barwo/preface.shtml.

Wertz, R. R. (2016). *Entertainment-Chinese Opera.* Retrieved October 21, 2020, from www.ibiblio.org/chineseculture/contents/entr/p-entr-c01s03.html.

Yang, J., Luo, J. M., & Lai, I. K. W. (2021). Construction of Leisure Consumer Loyalty from Cultural Identity—A Case of Cantonese Opera. *Sustainability,* 13(4), 1980.

Yao, J. (2020). 世界各地的八和会馆. Retrieved December 26, 2020, from www.gzzxws.gov.cn/qxws/lwws/lwzj/lwwsd9j/201410/t20141014_35001.htm.

Zhang, J. (2007). Comparison of Chinese Opera and Western Opera. *Drama Literature,* 10, 78–80.

Zhang, J. (2018). Research on the Development and Application of Kindergarten Curriculum Based on Traditional Chinese Culture. *Creative Education,* 9, 280–284. doi: 10.4236/ce.2018.92018.

Zhong, Z. P. 钟哲平 (2014).旧上海, 粤剧夜夜笙歌之地. 南国红豆 (6), 51–53.

Zhong, Z. P. 鍾哲平 (2015). 粵劇為何能漂洋過海傳到美國. Retrieved December 25, 2020, from https://read01.com/zh-hk/3Bdgm6.html#.X-W7bNgzZPY.

Zhuhai College of Jilin University. (2020). 傳承發展粵劇保護大灣區共同文化遺產. Retrieved November 4, 2020, from www.gangaonet.com/zhusanjiao/2020/0427/167549.html.

2 Development of Cantonese Opera in the Greater Bay Area

2.1 Cantonese Opera in Hong Kong

2.1.1 Development of Cantonese Opera in Hong Kong

Before the days of pop concerts, music festivals and Netflix, Cantonese opera was one of Hong Kong's most popular forms of entertainment. This genre, which falls within the wide range of Chinese opera, combines music, dance and art. It is often enjoyed on the stage of a dimly lit theatre.

China has more than 400 xiqu genres, and 14 of these xiqu genres are found in Guangdong. Cantonese opera is one of them. As people in China become highly mobile, Cantonese opera has not only spread within China but also all over the world. Hong Kong was a British colony before 1997. However, most of the population in Hong Kong is Cantonese because it is geographically close to Guangdong. Hence, both Hong Kong and Guangdong share similar cultures and traditions. These characteristics allow Cantonese opera to become a significant cultural activity in Hong Kong (EdUHK, 2021).

In the 19th century, Cantonese opera had two primary contexts. The first was ritual performance, which is usually held during gods' birthdays, festivals or other rituals. The venue is temporary and is usually built with bamboo and iron sheets. This important type of performance has a long history in Hong Kong. The second was theatre performance, which did not appear until theatres were built in the urban areas. This type of performance is usually performed in a theatre. In contrast to ritual performance, theatre performance is highly regular, commercial and entertaining. Hence, it attracts many audiences and provides huge profits by ticket sales. This type of performance is a contemporary development of Cantonese opera.

As the Cantonese dialect gradually replaced the Jungchau dialect in Hong Kong, Cantonese opera developed rapidly during the 1920s and 1930s. Many new scripts were written and many excellent troupes, such as Xue Jue Xian's Kok Sin Sing Opera Troupe and Ma Sze Tsang's Tai Ping Opera

DOI: 10.4324/9781003157564-2

Troupe, performed many traditional classics and new plays with outstanding costumes, music, stage design and acting styles. During the Second World War, many Cantonese opera professionals escaped from China to Hong Kong and Macau. This scenario lead to varied development of Cantonese opera in different areas. In Hong Kong, many Cantonese operas started performing in theatres or temporary theatres. However, many Cantonese opera troupes moved their performance to the big screen, and many excellent films were developed. Hence, theatres were used not only for Cantonese opera but also for film showings. In the beginning, most theatres were fully occupied by opera or films associated with big or successful troupes because the theatres' profit is directly associated with ticket sales. Many small troupes did not have much opportunity to perform. However, many amusement parks, such as those in Lai Chi Kok, Kai Tak and Tsuen Wan, were developed in the 1950s to 1960s. The theatres in these amusement parks and the reopening of the Hong Kong City Hall in 1962 provided ample opportunities for small troupes to practice and perform. Many town halls and community halls had developed with the progress of new towns in Hong Kong. These halls also provided sufficient venues for Cantonese opera troupes to perform. This scenario built the foundation which lead to the Golden Age of Cantonese opera in Hong Kong (EdUHK, 2021). Table 2.1 shows Cantonese opera performance venues and their corresponding capacity in Hong Kong.

Given that the number of troupes allowed to perform in different theatres in Hong Kong increased, the development of Cantonese opera during this period was remarkable. For example, the Chinese Artists Association of Hong Kong (or more commonly, Pak Wo Association) was established in 1953 to enhance and promote Cantonese opera. However, Cantonese opera had received a sudden drop of attention from the late 1960s until the late 1970s. More recently, the development of Cantonese opera has become promising because of the abundant amount of audience and theatres. Many new and amateur Cantonese opera associations were established. For example, the Hong Kong Arts Development Council (HKADC), a legal entity, was established in 1995 to direct, advertise and support art development in Hong Kong. HKADC also initiated the Xiqu Education Project to achieve its objective by introducing Cantonese opera to the new generation and encouraging the new generation to participate. In addition, after the HKADC had taken up the Arts Development Fund (or the Cultural Exchange Project), it assessed the application of local art organisations and provided subsidies. Local artists and art groups can continue to submit applications for eligible overseas cultural exchange projects to the Project Grant (Cultural Exchange) under HKADC (2021). In Hong Kong, Cantonese opera elements are displayed in many aspects of citizens' daily lives. For example, the note-issuing banks in Hong Kong incorporated a theme of

Cantonese opera on the reverse side of the 100 dollar note to act in concert with the Hong Kong Spirit initiated by the Hong Kong Monetary Authority. A coherent theme appeared on the bank notes issued by three different banks for the first time (see Figure 2.1).

2.1.2 *Major Stakeholders of Cantonese Opera in Hong Kong*

1) *Cantonese Opera Advisory Committee (COAC) and Cantonese Opera Development Fund (CODF)*

In 2004, the COAC was established to develop Cantonese opera effectively into unique local art. The COAC consists of the chairman, vice-chairman, members from the Pak Wo Association and many Cantonese opera-related professionals. The COAC provides recommendations and advice to the Secretary for Home Affairs to promote, preserve and develop Cantonese opera. The COAC regularly holds meetings, such as consultative meetings, or sharing sessions with the industry community to seek new ideas to promote Cantonese opera.

The CODF, a fund managed by the CODF Advisory Committee and sponsored by the Secretary for Home Affairs, was set up in 2005. The fund aims to assist programmes or events whose objective is to promote continuous and sustainable development of Cantonese opera. Starting in 2007, the CODF has received three rounds of application annually. All Cantonese opera-related programmes, such as professional training and performances,

Figure 2.1 The 2018 Series 100 HKD Note

Table 2.1 Cantonese Opera Performance Venues in Hong Kong

Name	Venue	Capacity (seats)	Tel:
Hong Kong City Hall	Theatre	463	29212821
Hong Kong City Hall	Concert hall	1,430	29212840
Hong Kong Cultural Centre	Grand Theatre	1,734	27342849
Hong Kong Cultural Centre	Concert hall	2,019	27342009
Kwai Tsing Theatre	Auditorium	905	24067505
Ko Shan Theatre	Theatre	1,031	23305261
Sha Tin Town Hall	Auditorium	1,372	26942550
Sai Wan Ho Civic Centre	Theatre	1,424	31845777
Tsuen Wan Town Hall	Auditorium	1,424	24937463
Sheung Wan Civic Centre	Auditorium	480	28532678
Tai Po Civic Centre	Auditorium	1,313	26654477
Tuen Mun Town Hall	Auditorium	1,372	24507875
Yuen Long Theatre	Auditorium	923	24771462
The Ngau Chi Wan Civic Centre	Theatre	354	27260973
North District Town Hall	Auditorium	500	26714400
Queen Elizabeth Stadium		3,500	23557282
Hong Kong Coliseum		12,000	23557261

(*Sources*: Leisure and Cultural Service Department (LCSD), HKSAR, 2020)

arts education and community activities, research and archival projects and cultural exchange and venue support projects proposed by locally registered bodies and individuals, are eligible for consideration.

In 2018–2019, the CODF received extra government funding. The CODF not only expanded its funding scope to cover many areas but also raised the funding ceiling for various items following the injection. The areas covered included encouraging the premieres and reruns of newly written Cantonese opera works, enhancing community or school activities to promote Cantonese opera and encouraging local troupes to stage Cantonese opera performances in the Mainland or overseas often. At the end of the year, the CODF provided $14 million subsidies to support roughly 60 Cantonese opera-related programmes, including the Venue Partnership Scheme initiated by the Pak Wo Association. The Association organised many events, rehearsals and training sessions for budding artists and students to nurture new talents and promote Cantonese opera (COAC-CODF, 2021).

2) *The Chinese Artists Association of Hong Kong*

The Chinese Artists Association of Hong Kong has been established for more than 130 years. It is a professional organisation for Cantonese opera professionals in Guangdong. Before the association formally registered its name in 1953, it was formerly known as The Chinese Actors' Association,

Association for the Development of Cantonese Opera and the Guangdong Professional Union for Cantonese Opera Performers.

The Pak Wo Association primarily aims to develop the art of traditional Cantonese opera. However, the association also has missions to protect the rights and welfare of the corresponding stakeholders, take care of the elderly and disabled and respect the Chinese saints. The Association has been very active in achieving its missions over the past 50 years. For example, whenever a natural disaster occurs in Hong Kong or mainland China, the association voluntarily organises fundraising activities, such as Loving Heart for the Disaster Victims, Warmth for Taiwan, Loving Heart for South Asia and Together to Warm Sichuan. The Association was officially registered as a charitable organisation in 2008. At present, the association represents more than 1,000 Cantonese opera performers in Hong Kong (The Chinese Artists Association of Hong Kong, 2021).

The Association had its inaugural co-operation with the Hong Kong Book Fair 2018 organised by the Hong Kong Trade Development Council. Audiences can obtain a deep understanding and enjoyment of the beauty of Cantonese opera through exhibition, excerpt performances and talks. The Association has organised an exhibition, A Gem of Chinese Culture – Cantonese Opera, in the Art Gallery. The exhibition introduces the history of Barwo and its effort in the promotion, education and preservation of Cantonese opera. The display area showcases invaluable Cantonese opera scripts, leaflets, photos of renowned Cantonese opera practitioners and journals. Moreover, the eminent Cantonese opera artists, Mr. Yuen Siu Fai and Mr. Wan Yuk Yu, lend their costumes specifically for Wai To and Hon Lung, respectively, for the special showcase.

3) The Hong Kong Academy for Performing Arts (HKAPA)

The HKAPA is a leading education institution of performing arts in Asia. It was established in 1984 by government ordinance. It provides undergraduate and postgraduate education, including Chinese opera, dance, drama, film and television, music and theatre and entertainment arts. This institution mainly focuses on the cultural diversity between the Chinese and Western cultures and interdisciplinary learning. Cantonese opera is a complex performing art combining singing, acting, dancing, movement, choreography and acrobatics. Thus, the Academy provides the first Cantonese opera degree in the world to educate the new generations and preserve this valuable Chinese culture. The Academy has been nurturing new talents in the Cantonese opera industry ever since its establishment. Many graduates have found placement in local professional Cantonese opera troupes or established their own troupes or production companies (HKAPA, 2021).

Some companies and troupes, for example, the Young Academy Cantonese Opera Troupe, gain popularity. This troupe was established in 2011. Moreover, this troupe primarily aims to provide practical training to young talents and preserve this traditional cultural art. Cantonese opera students are allowed to participate in the actual art and musical performance. Students are expected to participate frequently after the Xiqu Centre in West Kowloon Cultural District opens.

In 2009, Cantonese opera was officially included in the New Secondary School Curriculum. Hence, the demand for Cantonese opera educators increased dramatically. Some of the graduates from the Academy became educators and provided courses, seminars and extracurricular activities to local students. This arrangement increased not only the job opportunities for the Academy's graduates but also the number of future audiences by introducing Cantonese opera to the younger generations.

2.1.3 Current Issues of Cantonese Opera in Hong Kong

Hong Kong is never considered a city with a profound cultural background (Wong et al., 1997). The number of cultural events in Hong Kong is abundant, but the participation rate is only approximately 50% (Chau, 2014). This scenario shows that Hong Kong fails to develop itself as a city of arts. After Hong Kong returned to China in 1997, nurturing and preserving Chinese culture became an important issue. Cantonese opera is included in the UNESCO Intangible Cultural Heritage List. Thus, Cantonese opera has positioned its cultural and artistic status. At present, Cantonese opera is incorporated in the curriculum of Chinese language, general studies and music. The incorporation of Cantonese opera into extracurricular activities can be found in many situations. However, the transmission and preservation of Cantonese opera are considered in danger as many famous Cantonese opera performers are retired, and the new performers cannot attract the attention of the audience.

Music is usually not the priority in the primary and secondary education in Hong Kong. Many music teachers do not have sufficient Cantonese opera knowledge; hence, they cannot inspire the interest of the younger generations (Yu, 2001). In addition, some traditional and influential culture and art activities, such as May Fourth Movement, are considered outdated. Furthermore, most of the Hong Kong people are highly influenced by Western culture. Although many people in Hong Kong still enjoy traditional music and arts, the younger generation generally loses confidence in the attractiveness of the traditional arts (Yu, 2001; Lo, 2017). Traditional Chinese culture can no longer maintain its prestigious status (Ma, 2001).

Aside from the undergraduate degrees mentioned earlier, the HKAPA also provides diplomas and certificates for traditional theatre programmes to satisfy practical and theoretical needs. Although most students are admitted at around the age of 17, the starting age is relatively late from the traditional Cantonese opera training (master – disciple) perspective (Chau, 2013). Many educational institutions in mainland China offer vocal training to students before age 12. The traditional master – disciple type of training has become extinct and the only full-time training of Cantonese opera can be found in one tertiary institution because both students and teachers should exert enormous effort and time to master Cantonese opera. In addition, many custom rules within the Cantonese opera industry prohibit the development of Cantonese opera. For example, no official employment contract exists between the troupes and the staff and actors. This kind of arrangement does not reduce workers' commitment and does not fit the social environment today, which advocates a systematic structure and responsibility. Cantonese opera must make serious changes to conform to modern society.

2.2 Cantonese Opera in Macau

2.2.1 Development of Cantonese Opera in Macau

Cantonese opera has a long history in Macau. The first theatre in Macau, Cheng Peng Theatre, was built in 1875. *Cheng Peng* in Chinese means long and lasting peace and prosperity. This theatre is originally an important venue of Cantonese opera. In 1925, it also screened films. However, as Cantonese opera gradually lost its popularity in the 1990s, the theatre was shut down in 1992 (Macao Government Tourism Office, 2021a).

Cantonese opera is a favourite culture and art of Macao people, particularly the older generation of Macao residents, in the old days when not much entertainment was available. In the past, Cantonese opera was often performed in theatres. Many troupes, especially some well-known theatre troupes and famous actors and actresses, performed Cantonese opera in theatres. From the 1940s to the 1970s, many famous Guangzhou and Hong Kong actors, such as Hung Sin Nui, Yam Kim Fai, Pak Suet Sin, Fong Yim-fun, Sun Ma Sze Tsang, Fung Wong Nui, Leung Sing Poh and Lam Kar Sing, came to Macau to perform Cantonese opera in theatres. Cheng Peng Theatre was famous for its frequent performances by famous Cantonese opera actors. Next to the theatre is an herbal tea shop, and the herbal tea sold is named after Cantonese operas or famous actors.

Macau shares many things with Hong Kong and China. The performance of Cantonese opera is no exception. Cantonese opera is usually performed during traditional festivals, such as Entertaining People and Entertaining God and God and People. Cantonese opera was the best entertainment for Macau residents' daily life. Many people, both elderly and young, came together to watch Cantonese opera in ritual and theatre performances. From the 1940s to the 1960s, four professional female artists, including Leung Yuen Fong, Chiang Yim Hung, Cheng Pui-man and Tai Chi-kwan, famous for singing the Pinhou (natural voice), appeared in Macau. Cheng Pui-man is the only classics artist in Macau. The classics should be sung in Guilin vernacular – a feature that allows it to be consistent with the ancient pieces by sharing the same dialect.

Macau Cantonese opera also has its own characteristics. The local cultural elements are compatible with Chinese and Western cultures, and the nonconventional audience group provides opportunities for young actors to emerge. Around the 1940s, many Cantonese opera repertoires were adapted from dramas. Thus, the dialogue and performance style of the script had the characteristics of a drama, and the stage art emphasised novelty. Moreover, the Macanese in Macau still sing Cantonese opera in Portuguese. At present, many amateur Cantonese opera performances are held in Macau, giving Cantonese opera a solid folk foundation, a new way for Cantonese opera to exist beyond professional performance. Nowadays, more than two ritual performances and theatre performances are available for residents to watch each year.

Since the 1980s, the Macao and Portuguese authorities have also implemented a policy 'focusing on tourism and trade, supplemented by the service industry' in addition to continuing to open up the gaming industry. They paid much attention to Chinese culture and local culture and held events, such as the Macao Arts Festival. Cantonese opera was often performed. On the eve of Macau's return, according to statistics, dozens of Cantonese opera groups were present, most of which were amateurs. The main Cantonese opera groups include the Macao General Association of Cantonese Opera, Macao Lai Chon Chinese Opera Association, Cantonese Opera Juvenile's Troupe of General Union of Neighbors' Association of Macao and Macao Kaifong Cantonese Opera Juvenile's Troupe.

2.2.2 Major Stakeholders of Cantonese Opera in Macau

1) Alegria Cinema

The Alegria Cinema has been established in Macau for more than 60 years by a group of Chinese merchants. It is located at Travessa da Corda and Estrada do Repouso of the San Kio area. It had only 800 seats when it opened in 1952. Several years later, the number of seats increased to roughly 1,200, which offers approximately the same number of seats as UA Galaxy Cinemas. The group of Chinese merchants who built the Alegria Cinema was led by Ho Yin, a prominent social figure. Mr. Ho saw the need to increase national patriotism. He and a group of Chinese merchants provided the funding to build the cinema. Upon its completion, the Algeria Cinema became the first movie theatre to show patriotic films produced by mainland China. Many Hong Kong people travel to Macau for the sake of these films. Later on, films produced by other Communist countries, such as the Soviet Union, North Korea and Vietnam, were also shown (Macao Government Tourism Office, 2021b).

During the Cultural Revolution (1960–1970), many famous movies adapted from Chinese opera, namely, *The Legend of the Red Lantern*, *White-haired Girl* and *Red Detachment of Women*, were screened in the cinema. In the 1980s, as movie entertainment became much more popular, films produced by the United States and Hong Kong movie producers dominated the market. Most of the films in Macau were produced by the Great Wall Film Production, Feng Huang Motion Picture, Shaw Brothers Studio and Sun Luen Film Company. In addition, *Shaolin Temple*, a film starred in by Jet Li, received much attention. In the late 1990s, the cinema theatre conducted a series of changes. The original setup of movie theatres included the ground floor and the first floor. Compared with the ground floor, the first floor is higher and has a better view; thus, the price for the first floor is higher than that for the ground floor. However, during this period, the first floor was modified into an individual but small screening room whilst the ground floor remained. This setup allowed the theatres to show several movies simultaneously. On 22 December 2011, the Alegria Cinema began to show 3D movies.

The Alegria Cinema can accommodate a large number of guests. Thus, it was also used to hold community activities and Cantonese opera performances. Many famous Cantonese opera troupes, such as Chor Fung Ming Cantonese Opera Troupes, and many famous Cantonese opera artists, such as Lam Kar Sing, have performed in the Alegria Cinema. The cinema also provides a venue to many local singing associations and local communities, for example, National Day celebrations, table tennis tournaments, chess games, acrobatic shows and hard-qigong presentations, in addition to Cantonese opera. It is also the venue for many primary and secondary schools' graduation ceremonies and a very popular place for engagement or wedding parties (see Figure 2.2).

2) Cheng Peng Theatre

The Cheng Peng Theatre was the first theatre in Macau. *Cheng Peng* in Chinese means peace and prosperity. It was opened in 1875 with orchestra stalls, stages and dressing rooms. Fifty years later, it began to screen films, and the first film was *The White Sister*. The theatre switched back and forth between film screening and Cantonese opera performances during the 1940s to 1970s. The latest switch was in 1970, and the theatre was renovated in Art Deco style to screen film. However, the theatre closed in 1992 because of poor maintenance and management (Macao Government Tourism Office, 2021a).

Figure 2.2 Alegria Cinema (Macau)

The theatre was left unused for many years. Although it was later used as a parking garage, many interior decorations were preserved. The government has already made structural fixes to the theatre, which is now undergoing interior decoration, to preserve its historical value and cultural functions. When it reopens, it will include a small Cantonese opera museum, cultural and creative space and performance practice room so that residents and visitors can learn the history of Cantonese opera (see Figure 2.3).

3) The Macau General Association of Cantonese Opera

Cantonese opera is an intangible asset that is inscribed on the UNESCO Intangible Cultural Heritage List. The Macau General Association of Cantonese Opera is an association uniting stakeholders in Cantonese opera communities to promote and preserve Cantonese opera, so that Cantonese opera can be passed down and flourish. For example, the local production of *Tale of the Pipa* features distinguished performers from Hong Kong and mainland China, reasserting Macau's identity as an important centre of Chinese culture.

In the past, the association promoted and exchanged Cantonese opera art, organised various performance activities and assisted the affiliated associations in opening up the conference affairs and achieving certain results.

Figure 2.3 Cheng Peng Theatre (Macau)

In the future, it will also organise Cantonese opera training classes as planned to promote Cantonese opera development. It hopes to attract fans, improve the artistic level and further promote Cantonese opera development (Macao General Association of Cantonese Opera, 2021).

2.2.3 *Current Issues of Cantonese Opera in Macau*

Cantonese opera was extremely popular in Macau during the mid-20th century. Many famous Cantonese opera celebrities, such as Yam Kim Fai and Pak Suet Sin, staged regular performances in Macau (Io & Chong, 2020). Since then, many have considered Cantonese opera the most popular genre of performing arts in Macau in the last century (Zhang, 2010). Although the popularity of Cantonese opera in Macau has been gradually decreasing, many loyal fans and more than 200 performing groups of Cantonese opera remain active in Macau (Io, 2019). Cantonese opera is frequently featured on TV, radio, the Internet and some local festivals in Macau, in addition to its regular performances. Some teenager-oriented Cantonese opera classes have been introduced in the recent decade to cultivate young Cantonese opera fans and artists. However, the majority of the local audiences are still older residents. The decrease in Cantonese opera's younger fans challenges Cantonese opera's sustainability in Macau (Io, 2019).

In Hong Kong and Guangzhou, many organisations and academies cooperated to cultivate talents in Cantonese opera by setting up courses. Compared with those of Hong Kong and Guangzhou, Macau's preservation and development of Cantonese opera and cultivation of young talents are far inferior. The government and the public should cooperate reasonably in the future to integrate the inherited Cantonese opera art and culture and carry it forward.

2.3 Cantonese Opera in Guangdong Province

2.3.1 Development of Cantonese Opera in Guangdong Province

The development of Cantonese opera in Guangdong can be traced back to the Ming dynasty. Some local operas incorporated several classes of performance, such as yiyang, bangzi, pihuang and kunqu, into Cantonese opera. However, many opera troupes from the north moved to Guangdong during the Qing dynasty. These troupes, usually considered much cultivated, were widely accepted by the elite in the Guangdong community. This progress marked the starting point of Cantonese opera development.

Cantonese opera developed rapidly after the People's Republic of China (PRC) was established. The colourful drama creation, which advocates the legacy and development of the singing genre of artistic predecessors, enhances the artistic charm of generous singing and shallow singing; the accompaniment music supports the combination of Chinese and Western music and strives to highlight the national and local characteristics. Cantonese opera development includes establishing a director system, purifying the image of stage art, paying much attention to the overall art and designing stage variety. As Cantonese opera became much popular in Guangdong, Zhou Enlai, the first premier of the PRC, named Cantonese Opera the Red Bean of Southern Country. Tian Han, a great dramatist, praised Cantonese opera for its artistic characteristics of 'passion like fire, lingering melancholy'.

At present, 73 professional Guangdong Opera troupes remain. The first Cantonese opera troupe in Guangzhou (the capital of Guangdong) was developed in 1953. Five years later, several troupes combined to form the Guangdong Cantonese Opera Troupe. In 1960, Guangdong Cantonese Opera School and its Zhanjiang Branch were established. Many famous actors and actresses, such as Xue Jue Xian, Ma Sze Tsang, Bai Jurong, Luo Pinchao and Hung Sin Nui, starred in various plays, such as *Guan Hanqing*, *Liu Yi Biography* and *Shanxiang Fengyun*. Amongst the plays mentioned, *Shanxiang Fengyun* can be considered one of the most successful plays. This play has been recreated into more than 20 different plays in China and played in North Korea and Vietnam. The famous artists mentioned earlier also demonstrate various singing styles in Cantonese opera, for example,

Ma Sze Tsang's 'beggar throat' singing, Bai Jurong's 'flat throat' and the 'red tune' of Hung Sin Nui. In the 1980s, many new plays, such as *Princess Zhaojun* and *Empress Li of the Southern Tang Dynasty*, and many new actors, such as Guan Guohua, Lin Jinping, Lu Qiuping, Ni Huiying, Feng Gangyi, Ding Fan, Guo Fengnu, Chen Yunhong, Peng Chiquan and Cao Xiuqin, appeared (TravelChina1.com, 2019).

Since Cantonese opera was listed in the Intangible Cultural Heritage List in 2009, the local government has paid considerable attention to its protection and inheritance. A series of explorations on the legislative protection of Cantonese opera culture has also been made to ensure the preservation and development of Cantonese opera. In 2014, the Guangdong government established legislation to protect Cantonese opera, and the local government announced that it would establish a Cantonese opera teaching system and a complete Cantonese opera database. In 2016, the Guangdong Provincial Department of Culture investigated and researched the legislation of Cantonese opera to perfect and complete the Guangdong Provincial Provisions for Protection Management on Cantonese opera (from now on referred to as 'Provisions'). The Provisions, approved by the People's Government of Guangdong Province in 2017, provided a legal guarantee for the protection and inheritance of Cantonese opera. In 2018, the Ministry of Education awarded the two education institutions, Guangdong Opera Heritage Base of South China University of Technology and Guangdong Opera Heritage Base of Xinghai Conservatory of Music, the first batch of excellent traditional Chinese culture heritage bases.

2.3.2 *Major Stakeholders of Cantonese Opera in Guangdong Province*

1) *Guangdong Yueju Opera Theatre*

As a complement to the development of the Guangdong Cantonese Opera Troupe, the Guangdong Yueju Opera Theater was built when the said troupe was established (Guangdong Yueju Opera Theater, 2021). The theatre nurtures many famous artists, such as Ma Sze Tsang, Hung Sin Nui, Luo Pin Chao and Bai Jurong. Famous performers, such as Ding Fan, Chen Yunhong, Cao Xiuqin and Wu Guohua, have successively won the Plum Blossom Award for Chinese Opera. Ding Fan and Chen Yunhong also won the Wenhua Award for performance issued by the Ministry of Culture.

The theatre has two troupes. The troupes perform not only in China but also in many places outside of the country, such as Vietnam, the United States, Canada, Australia, Singapore, Malaysia, Taiwan, Hong Kong and Macau. The theatre also produces many classical plays, such as *Searching the Academy*, *Guan Hanqing* and *Shanxiang Fengyun*, and many contemporary plays, such as *Forty Years of Broken Dreams*, *Unforgettable Zhujiang Alley*, *Legend of Lun Wenqin* and *Lady Umbrella*. *Unforgettable Zhujiang* and *Legend of Lun Wenqin* won the Wenhua Award for New Repertoire. *Legend of Lun Wenqin* also won the Guangdong Lu Xun Literature Award. *Lady Umbrella* won the Best Play Award at the 5th Chinese Opera Festival and the Silver Prize of the Peacock Award.

2) Artists Association of Guangdong (Pak Wo Association)

The Artists Association of Guangdong was initially developed as a community to connect Cantonese opera artists. However, the association was later banned by the Qing dynasty in 1854 because of its involvement in the Taiping Rebellion. After the ban was lifted in the 1880s, some artists built a mansion at Huangsha, which can accommodate more than 1,000 people. This development made the modern Artists Association of Guangdong and Huangsha prosperous and gave rise to bustling attractions in Guangdong. Unfortunately, the mansion in Huangsha was later destroyed by the Japanese during the Second World War, and the association was rebuilt after the war was over. The new mansion is not as magnificent as the previous one, but it has continued to connect many artists. It eventually preserved many posters, photos and collections of many famous artists in Guangdong and Hong Kong.

The Artists Association of Guangdong has branches in many countries of the world. In places where Cantonese-speaking Chinese are present, the branches of the association are said to exist as well. With the profound historical and cultural implications of Guangdong, the Artists Association of Guangdong enjoys a high status and is usually considered the birthplace of Cantonese opera (see Figure 2.4).

3) Cantonese Opera Art Museum

The Cantonese Opera Art Museum in the Liwan District of Guangzhou City, south China's Guangdong Province, was built in 2016. Cantonese opera and Lingnan culture are closely connected in this area. The Guangzhou government built this museum to support the endangered Cantonese opera. The museum is more than 15,000 square metres. People can watch craftspeople carve olive pits, paint porcelain, fashion guqin and Wing Chun kung fu (Yuejuopera.org.cn, 2021).

The museum contains many collections, such as costumes, dresses and masks used by famous artists. The total number of collections exceeds 5,000. The museum also provides free shows on both outdoor and indoor stages to visitors. In addition to the performance, the buildings or theatre inside the

Figure 2.4 Artists Association of Guangdong (Foshan)

museum is an attraction. For example, Hexiang Building, the highest build-ing in the museum, is constructed based on the nostalgic style of the 1930s. A desirable feature is the extremely long curtain (7 meters) in the theatre.

Tourists can enjoy theme exhibitions and Cantonese opera performances in nearly every corner inside the museum. Audiovisual studios and reading rooms are also available for visitors to enjoy the opera and check related information. At the costume display area, various beautiful Cantonese opera costumes are exhibited. Visitors can watch vivid images through a touch-screen. The Cantonese Opera Art Museum attempts to preserve the tradi-tional art culture in today's world, in its birthplace and land (see Figure 2.5).

2.3.3 Current Issues of Cantonese Opera in Guangdong Province

Cantonese opera talents have gradually disappeared in the new genera-tion. Today's Cantonese opera exhibits a temporary shortage of talents, and relevant skills are on the verge of being lost. Thus, Cantonese opera is in a no-successor situation. The young generations born after the 1980s and 1990s tend to be attracted by the 'fast-food culture' prevalent in the new era. They rarely possess a strong interest in Cantonese opera culture and are

Figure 2.5 Cantonese Opera Art Museum (Guangzhou)

hardly willing to learn Cantonese opera performances. This situation worsens with the successive deaths of many outstanding Cantonese opera artists from older generations. In addition to this adversity, people have been offered many alternative sources of entertainment as society continues to develop. This scenario is especially true with the younger generation when new forms of media are developed. Young people feel that they are alienated from this culture. This view is probably the fundamental reason why Cantonese opera is endangered.

The government does not pay enough attention, and the investment is insufficient. Firstly, the government does not give capital support to Cantonese opera development. The salary of a Cantonese opera performer is generally around 3,000 Yuan, and being such a performer requires a large amount of Cantonese opera skills and experience. However, the salary of an ordinary migrant worker at present is also almost 3,000 Yuan; thus, many people give up the opportunity to engage in Cantonese opera. Secondly, the government fails to provide a good external environment for Cantonese opera development. Cantonese opera troupes cannot earn a living with the current number of performances; hence, the troupes cannot retain talents (Mei et al., 2018).

The inheritance of culture should firstly begin with school education. Schools can educate students based on innovative teaching thoughts and realistic teaching attitudes. In addition, schools may create a set of body figure exercises suitable for students to exercise Cantonese opera in combination with the physical and mental development characteristics of students. The materials for creating Cantonese opera on campuses should be selected based on innovative thinking and to the extent that the programmes created and rehearsed are suitable for students to understand and learn. The Cantonese opera *Nanguo Hongdou* has been absorbed in the current music textbooks in Guangdong Province, enabling local students to enhance their understanding of local traditional culture. In addition, schools should also organise relevant knowledge contests and arrange activities for students including watching Cantonese opera to enhance students' interest in Cantonese opera and directly introduce Cantonese opera music on campuses. Moreover, schools may also provide a second classroom, where Cantonese opera masters can give lectures to sow Cantonese opera seeds on campuses (Lo, 2017).

2.4 Summary

Cantonese opera was initially developed in Guangdong, but it has spread to the rest of the world. Despite being colonies before, Hong Kong and Macau are geographically close to Guangdong, and the majority of the population are Cantonese. Thus, Cantonese opera can gain from the best features of Hong Kong and Macau and establish itself as one of the major cultural activities in these areas.

Cantonese opera is a valuable heritage not only to Cantonese but also to all Chinese. During the last decade, Cantonese opera has become endangered because of the changes in people's habits and preferences. The central and local government and local communities used different methods to preserve this valuable culture. For example, all governments allocated many resources to education by incorporating Cantonese opera into the school curriculum. These actions aim to inspire and enhance younger people's aesthetic perspective and increase their interest in the future development of Cantonese opera.

References

Chau, W. (2013). *Deciding the Future of Cantonese Opera*. Retrieved January 11, 2021, from www.scmp.com/lifestyle/arts-culture/article/1202590/deciding-future-cantonese-opera.

Chau, W. (2014). *Arts Audiences Grow but Old Problems Remain*. Retrieved January 11, 2021, from www.scmp.com/news/hong-kong/article/1652525/arts-audiences-grow-old-problems-remain.

The Chinese Artists Association of Hong Kong. (2021). *Introduction*. Retrieved January 11, 2021, from www.hkbarwo.com/aboutus_aim.php.

COAC-CODF. (2021). *Cantonese Opera Development Fund*. Retrieved January 11, 2021, from www.coac-codf.org.hk/en/codf/index.html.

EdUHK. (2021). *Cantonese Opera (Yueju) in Hong Kong*. Retrieved March 11, 2021, from www.ied.edu.hk/ccaproject/yueju/eng/index_hk.php.

Guangdong Yueju Opera Theater. (2021). *Introduction*. Retrieved February 11, 2021, from www.gdyjy.com/gb/about0.asp?newsid=1.

The Hong Kong Academy for Performing Arts (HKAPA). (2021). *Chinese Opera*. Retrieved January 11, 2021, from www.hkapa.edu/co.

Hong Kong Arts Development Council (HKADC). (2021). *About HKADC*. Retrieved February 1, 2021, from www.hkadc.org.hk/?p=81&lang=en.

Io, M. U. (2019). Collaboration Between Practitioners and Public Agencies in Preserving and Promoting Musical Heritage in Macao. *Journal of Heritage Tourism*, 14(1), 19–32.

Io, M. U., & Chong, D. (2020). Determining Residents' Enjoyment of Cantonese Opera as Their Performing Arts Heritage in Macao. *Annals of Leisure Research*, 1–18.

Leisure and Cultural Service Department (LCSD), HKSAR (2021). *Facilities & Venues*. Received 11, January, 2021, from https://www.lcsd.gov.hk/en/.

Lo, W. H. (2017). Traditional Opera and Young People: Cantonese Opera as Personal Development. *International Journal of Adolescence and Youth*, 22(2), 238–249.

Ma, K. W. (2001). Peripheral Vision: Chinese Cultural Studies in Hong Kong. In T. Miller (Ed.), *A Companion to Cultural Studies* (pp. 259–274). Oxford: Blackwell.

Macao General Association of Cantonese Opera. (2021). *Tale of the Pipa*. Retrieved March 11, 2021, from www.icm.gov.mo/fam/26/en/eventdetail.aspx?id=5134.

Macao Government Tourism Office. (2021a). *Footsteps into the Historic Centre*. Retrieved January 11, 2021, from www.macaotourism.gov.mo/en/suggested-tours/footsteps-into-the-historic-centre#cheng-peng-theatre.

Macao Government Tourism Office. (2021b). *Shows*. Retrieved January 11, 2021, from www.macaotourism.gov.mo/en/shows-and-entertainment/shows/yueju-opera-cantonese-opera.

Mei, Y., Guo, M., Lin, M., Jiang, G., Zhou, J., Zhou, H., . . . Xie, M. (2018, December). Protection and Inheritance of Cantonese Opera. In *2nd International Conference on Art Studies: Science, Experience, Education (ICASSEE 2018)* (pp. 518–523). Dordrecht, The Netherlands: Atlantis Press.

TravelChina1.com. (2019). *Guangdong Opera*. Retrieved January 11, 2021, from www.travelchina1.com/thread/Guangdong-Opera-YueJu.html.

Wong, W. C., Chan, C. K., & Li, S. L. (Eds.). (1997). *Hong Kong Un-Imagined History: History, Culture and Future*. Taipei: Rye Field Publishing Company.

Yu, S. (2001). *Hong Kong High and Low Music Culture*. Hong Kong: Oxford University Press.

Yuejuopera.org.cn. (2021). *Information*. Retrieved January 11, 2021, from www.yuejuopera.org.cn/dtxx/fydtzx/.

Zhang, J. (2010). *Macau Opera*. Beijing: Culture and Art Publishing House.

3 Cantonese Opera as a Cultural Product

3.1 Cultural Product

Culture is a dynamic concept embedded in social, ethnic and heritage lifestyle. It involves human responses and developments in daily life, customs and traditions. It is an important concept in anthropology, including the phenomenon transmitted by social learning in human society. Cultural products include, but are not limited to, products made from textiles, wood, ceramics, glass and metal. These products demonstrate both aesthetic characteristics and technologies of the artisans' local traditions (Littrell & Miller, 2001). However, cultural products remain a vague concept. According to UNESCO, cultural products refer to 'the specificity of cultural goods and services, which, as vectors of identity, values, and meaning, must not be treated as mere commodities or consumer goods' (UNESCO, 2001).

As tourism becomes highly important in many destinations, culture becomes an important characteristic that differentiates one from the other. Hence, it also helps enhance and preserve the value of heritage. According to Richard (1996), cultural tourism includes consumption of goods and experiences; therefore, cultural tourism products can be used to observe cultural tourism value. The word *consumption* is highly controversial to many people because they mistakenly equate consumption with waste; hence, they classify it as destruction. However, cultural tourism has become very popular nowadays. Thus, it attracts many modern experiential tourists to travel around the world and participate in different interactive experiences. In addition, it initiates the destination, as well as tourism products providers, to create and develop new cultural products and to preserve and sustain the existing ones. This observation can make the economic development of culture and cultural heritage highly sustainable.

Cultural heritage is an expression of how people live traditionally. It includes customs, practices, places, objects, artistic expressions and values. It is usually classified into two types: tangible or intangible cultural

DOI: 10.4324/9781003157564-3

heritage (International Council on Monuments and Sites, 2002). According to UNESCO (2003a), tangible cultural heritage includes buildings and historical places, monuments and artefacts, which are considered worthy of preservation for the future. These objects are important heritage to archaeology, architecture, science or technology of a specific culture. Intangible cultural heritage includes what people have inherited from their ancestors, such as oral traditions, performing arts, social practices, rituals, festivals, knowledge and practices and skills to produce traditional crafts. Given that the world is highly globalised nowadays, intangible cultural heritage provides a way to preserve cultural diversity to understand dialogue amongst cultures and respect one another.

Cantonese opera is an essential member of Chinese opera. Although it originally came from Southern China, particularly Guangdong and Guangxi, it spread to Hong Kong, Macau and many other places in the world. In a certain respect, Cantonese opera is like many Chinese operas, such as the demonstration of martial arts and the involvement of singing, acting and acrobatics. Similarly, Cantonese opera usually involves Chinese history, culture, customs and philosophies. Following Kunqu, Cantonese opera was inscribed into the List of Intangible Cultural Heritage of Humanity in 2009.

3.2 Characteristics of Cantonese Opera

3.2.1 Dress and Makeup

In the old days, actors and actresses usually wore much makeup, but their dresses were relatively simple. Their dresses are usually based on five colours, red, black, white, blue and yellow, representing loyalty, honesty, cattiness, arrogance and capability, respectively. The makeup is usually consistent with the role played. However, starting in the 1920s, actors and actresses began to reduce the amount of makeup, and the most popular type was 'red-white face'.

Cantonese opera actors and actresses used different types of headwear, such as headgear, chignon and accessories, during their performance. Each headwear has unique characteristics. Therefore, it must be used and protected differently. Both actors and actresses use headwear, but actresses use headwear more frequently than actors. For example, the actor portraying Jia Baoyu usually wears a Taizi (prince) headwear in *A Dream of Red Mansion*. Headwear is only a part of Cantonese opera. Many Cantonese opera's historical backgrounds are Ming dynasty. Hence, the clothing of Cantonese opera demonstrates the characteristics of clothing in the Ming dynasty. Costumes can help establish the characteristics of the actors or actresses. For example, an actor needs to wear an outfit with long sleeves when he plays a gentle character, such as Xiaosheng; when he needs to portray a character such as Xiaowu, he needs to wear short sleeves.

Costume is only a part of Cantonese opera. Singing and acting are the most important skills, whereas martial arts and gymnastic skills also help deliver a performance. In the old days, Cantonese opera had very few female actresses. Therefore, most of the female roles were performed by actors. They must sing falsetto to perform as females. Acting refers to body language, gestures and walking style (see Figure 3.1).

3.2.2 Music

Similar to operas in Europe, Cantonese opera employs music and songs to perform. However, Cantonese opera focuses mainly on the singing, particularly the lyrics, instead of the music. Cantonese opera scriptwriters incorporate lyrics into music. Cantonese opera music is usually performed using Er wu (yee wu), Yangqin, Pipa and percussion. The percussion in Cantonese opera traditionally includes drums and cymbals. At present, the instruments used in Cantonese opera music includes cellos, saxophone and violin. More than 40 different types of musical instruments are used during Cantonese

Figure 3.1 Dress and Makeup of Cantonese Opera

opera performances. Although songs have different melodies and are played using various instruments, singers input their emotions and passion into songs with different personal styles (see Figure 3.2).

3.2.3 Types of Plays

Cantonese opera plays are usually classified into two major types: *Wu* (martial arts) plays, which traditionally emphasise war, and *Wen* (educated) plays, which usually emphasise poetry and culture. Wu plays usually contain

Figure 3.2 Music of Cantonese Opera

actions, weapons and armour. Hence, the characters are typically warriors. Wen plays are usually gentler and more elegant than Wu plays. Hence, the characters are generally scholars. Moreover, Wen plays are usually more dramatic with slower movements than Wu plays. Actors and actresses usually demonstrate their acting and performing skills via facial expression, tone of voice and water sleeves work, that is, the usage of sleeves on the costumes to produce water ripple types of movement. Acting in Cantonese opera is different from acting in TV or movies. In TV or movie acting, the camera can focus on a particular part of actors or actresses. However, in Cantonese opera acting, the emotion, body gesture and facial expressions must be delivered simultaneously. The actors and actresses do not have to keep acting with their water sleeves work. They should protect their histrionic makeup and costumes. In Wen plays, actors and actresses must also express their emotions via facial expressions. In general, Cantonese opera includes 10 principal roles, namely, Mo, Sheng, Dan, Jing, Chou, Wai, Xiao, Fu, Tie and Za. The actors and actresses must train and rehearse extensively to excel in these roles.

Cantonese opera not only entertains but also educates. Many Cantonese opera's scripts are about patriotism, family and friendship. They teach people to be loyal to the country and filial to their parents. Hence, Cantonese opera also serves the purpose of teaching morals and philosophy before formal education is available to the public. Therefore, the government heavily screens and examines the scripts and plays to ensure that the right messages are delivered. Lo (2015) found that Cantonese opera can help the elderly to connect with one another through a sense of collectivism and promote successful ageing. Some younger generations also found that Cantonese opera can help enhance their personal development (see Figure 3.3).

3.3 Cantonese Opera as Tourism Resources

3.3.1 *Intangible Cultural Heritage*

UNESCO (2003a) defines intangible cultural heritage as a subject including, but not limited to, practices, representations, expressions, knowledge and skills that people, community and groups recognise as a part of their culture. Performing arts, such as music, dance and opera, is a type of intangible cultural heritage because it possesses many cultural expressions, which are treasures of human creativity (UNESCO, 2003b). Historical and cultural development can be easily understood by the general public, including people from different cultures, via various platforms, such as music and dance (Mason, 2004; Xie & Lane, 2006; Fremaux & Fremaux, 2013; Xie et al., 2007). In addition, performing art not only is a cultural heritage but also can be used to develop

Figure 3.3 Types of Plays of Cantonese Opera

new tourism projects, such as museums of musicians and performing art events for tourists (Fremaux & Fremaux, 2013; Gapinski, 1988).

In recent years, intangible cultural heritage as a tourism product has received much attention from scholars (Ahmad, 2006; Park, 2011). Traditional performing arts promote the cultural identity and values of a place (Henke, 2005; Diettrich, 2015). Many scholars (Carnegie & McCabe, 2008; Poria et al., 2006) agree that authenticity is the most important experiential attribute in cultural heritage research. Whether a heritage is included in the list of world heritage affects the popularity and sustainability of a heritage (Hede, 2008). However, many scholars focus mainly on preserving and sustaining the heritage site, as well as its authenticity (Du Cros, 2007; Gilmore et al., 2007; De Rojas & Camarero, 2008). The research of the same or similar issues in performing arts is rare in the literature.

Intangible and tangible cultural heritage possess several similar experiential attributes, such as authenticity and educational experiences (Chhabra, 2010; Miichi, 2016). From the perspective of the local community, traditional performing arts are a part of the community's cultural identity, pride and history (Connell & Gibson, 2004; Van der Hoeven, 2012). However, as modern performing arts and new entertainment develop, people's interest in traditional performing arts lessens, making the development and preservation of traditional performing arts critical (UNESCO, 2003a). Its development and preservation cannot rely only on loyal fans. The support of the public is also essential (UNESCO, 2003a; Miichi, 2016). Public support not only helps preserve the heritage but also increases the number of audiences (Tikkanen, 2008; Diettrich, 2015). Although Cantonese opera is famous in many places, such as Hong Kong, Macau and many cities in China and Southeast Asia, local governments from Hong Kong, Macau and Guangdong applied for and successfully inscribed to UNESCO's Representative List of the Intangible Cultural Heritage of Humanity in 2009 (UNESCO, 2009). Following Kunqu Opera, Cantonese opera is the second Chinese opera inscribed on the list, and it is the only intangible asset from Guangdong that is inscribed (Guo & Li, 2015). Moreover, Cantonese opera is not only entertainment but also a collective memory for many people, especially the elderly, in Hong Kong, Macau and Guangdong (Macau Cultural Affairs Bureau, 2016). However, Cantonese opera is not popular with many non-Cantonese speaking people (UNESCO, 2009). In addition, the value of Cantonese opera as a tourism resource is not fully explored or utilised. The reasons include the lack of understanding of tourists' experiences and perception of Cantonese opera (Io, 2018).

As a valuable intangible cultural heritage, Cantonese opera has been performed widely in different festivals held in the Greater Bay Area (GBA), particularly in three major cities: Hong Kong, Macau and Guangzhou.

Hong Kong

The traditional performance called Opera for Deities refers to all the operas performed which aim to celebrate folk festivals, birthday of deities and establishment or renovations of altars and temples. The performance is believed to be shared by people and god. This kind of performance is not only a show but also a witness to a valuable historical culture, thereby helping people know much about the development of operas. Considerable research shows that most Cantonese operas in Hong Kong can be categorised as Operas for Deities. During popular festivals, Cantonese opera is performed not only to show respect to god and wish good luck but also to enrich people's spiritual life. The scale of a performance venue varies from 50 to 1,500. This valuable performance culture can also be inherited and promoted as an attractive tourism resource, given that cultural tourism has gained much popularity in recent years. However, some scholars determined that the fast urbanisation and demographic changes decrease the popularity of Opera for Deities because many people nowadays prefer to appreciate performance in modern cinemas instead of bamboo theatres. Therefore, as a culturally diverse city, Hong Kong must preserve and rejuvenate traditional operas to enhance their attractiveness, turning each performance into a new must-see attraction for tourists in the future.

Since 2010, Hong Kong has also been holding the Chinese Opera Festival (COF) annually, organised by the Leisure and Cultural Services Department. The festival usually lasts for 50 days. This annual event aims to bring the best of Chinese opera to the local stage by partnering with different organisations and individual performers. From this point of view, this festival can also be regarded as a cherished intangible cultural heritage. According to the director of the Arts Department of the Ministry of Culture, 'Xiqu is an important carrier of Chinese traditional culture, and Hong Kong is an international stage. Holding the Xiqu festival here can not only enhance the emotional exchanges between the people of Hong Kong and the Mainland, but also introduce more outstanding local operas from the Mainland to the rest of the world, helping the promotion of excellent Chinese traditional culture'. Compared with the ticket price in some major cities in mainland China, the ticket price in Hong Kong is relatively low, whilst the performance quality is high, gradually attracting many people to visit Hong Kong and see an opera performance. The Hong Kong Leisure and Cultural Services Department has recently cooperated with the Hong Kong Tourism Board (HKTB) actively. They try to attract many foreign tourists to come to Hong Kong during the COF. Therefore, seeing audiences with different skin colours in some theatres in Hong Kong is common.

Macau

Cantonese opera performance is also an indispensable part of many traditional festivals. For instance, on the day of the Tam Kong Festival, which is a traditional mega festival in Macau, Cantonese opera is performed as Opera for Deities in some bamboo theatres exclusively established for the performance Cultural Heritage of Macau. (n.d.). Similar to the case in Hong Kong, Opera for Deities also has a long history in Macau, attracting many residents and tourists every year. The Macau Art Festival also serves as a suitable carrier to promote Cantonese opera culture. In the 30th Macau Art Festival, The Soul of Macau is the closing programme of the festival. The Soul of Macau is based on a play originally written by a Macau scriptwriter. National first-class playwright Li Xinhua, together with the actors and actresses in Macau and Foshan Cantonese Opera Troupe, adapted the original script, presented the life of Macau and demonstrated the cultural connection within the Guangdong-Hong Kong-Macau GBA (Macau Travel Talk, 2019).

The 1st Guangdong-Hong Kong-Macau GBA Chinese Opera Cultural Festival was held in the Venetian Hotel from 5 to 9 November 2020. The event was also the first joint exhibition of Cantonese operas in the GBA. It increased people's national self-confidence and cultural identity and strengthened the connection between Chinese and Portuguese. In addition, the festival also elevated the Chinese culture to the world by demonstrating the soft power of Chinese culture (The Venetian Macau, 2020). Cantonese opera is undoubtedly one of the most classic forms of performance in the festival.

Guangzhou

Various festivals are held to inherit and promote Cantonese opera. Guangzhou Cantonese Opera Festival is a classic one. The Yangcheng Cantonese Opera Festival has been held since 1990. It is the largest, most influential and authoritative Cantonese opera cultural exchange brand in China. In the latest festival, 158 programmes from three countries, including the United States, Canada and New Zealand, and 38 organisations from Hong Kong, Macau and Guangdong in China, delivered 21 evening parties. This festival attracted more than 3,000 Cantonese opera performers and more than 20,000 audience members. The average occupancy rate was more than 70%. More than 18 million people saw the performance via an online platform (Xinhua News, 2020). In addition, Cantonese opera entered a city park where people can have their leisure activities by watching opera performances not only for the elderly but also for the children. Guangzhou Yuexiu Park integrated intangible Cantonese opera elements into a tangible place and cooperated with different social organisations to make this traditional performing art a unique tool to promote Lingnan culture. The red boat has always been a symbol of Cantonese opera. In 2016, Guangzhou recreated the Cantonese opera promotion carrier, the Pearl River Red Boat Theatre. Thus far, the theatre has performed more than 1,000 shows and received nearly 200,000 tourists from home and abroad. It has become a new business card for Guangzhou to spread Lingnan culture and Cantonese opera culture. Guangzhou Chuanshuo Children's Cultural Foundation stated that it will cooperate with Yuexiu Park to provide a platform for children's Cantonese opera to enter the society and make new contributions to the entry of intangible cultural heritage into scenic spots (China News, 2020a).

Practitioners may attach relevant, tangible souvenirs, games and exhibitions to the live performances of Cantonese opera to improve tourists' enjoyment of Cantonese opera and stimulate their interest in it. In addition to using easy-to-understand performance approaches, pre-performance workshops/seminars are recommended to help tourists understand and appreciate the artistic and cultural features of Cantonese opera. Moreover, destination managers can provide a wide variety of live performances to make tourists' consumption experience much more convenient. This effort can help stimulate tourists' interest in Cantonese opera (Lo, 2017).

3.3.2 Cantonese Opera Stars

The celebrity effect of Cantonese opera stars should not be ignored but made good use of to help further in promoting Cantonese opera as a tourism resource in the GBA. The following paragraphs introduce several Cantonese opera stars in both past and modern times.

Influences of Hung Sin Nui

Looking back to history, the stars who made remarkable contributions to Cantonese opera development are truly worth mentioning. Firstly, let us talk about Hung Sin Nui. Hung Sin Nui was born in 1925 in a family of Cantonese opera members. One of her relatives, Kuang Xinhua, was the founder of the Pak Wo Association. The year 1946 was important in the artistic career of Hung Sin Nui. In the spring of that year, she and her husband, Ma Sze Tsang, firstly co-acted in the opera *Give Me Back the Han Jiangshan* in Guangzhou. Before that, she had been on the mainland for more than two years. At that time, experts and audiences gave the following comments, 'She was young, good-looking, not meticulous enough, and promising'. In the second half of the same year, she performed in Hong Kong for a newly edited fashion drama, *I'm Crazy about You*. This drama had a strong line up, including Ma Sze Tsang, and the plot was close to the life of the people. The popularity was unprecedented. The audience became very familiar with Hung Sin Nui, who was not yet 20 years old at that time.

Then in 1947, Hung Sin Nui participated in three movies and two records, which marked her entry into the movie and music record fields, and she later became a famous star. In 1951, the word *Nu Qiang* or *Hong Qiang* appeared in a Hong Kong newspaper after she participated in Baofeng Cantonese Opera Association and performed *Yi Dai Tian Jiao*. Her growing influence made many Hong Kong residents notice her. A Hong Kong newspaper even reported that 'There are Hong Kong people who don't know about Queen of England, but there are no Hong Kong people [who] don't know about Hung Sin Nui', which further demonstrated her influence in Hong Kong at that time. Hung Sin Nui won the hearts of not only Hong Kong people but also the audience overseas. In her 60 years' career, she participated in more than 70 films and performed nearly 200 Cantonese operas. She also served as Folk Artist Ambassador, making a significant contribution in promoting and spreading Chinese opera culture to Southeast Asia and America.

In addition, during the time of 1950 to 1960, Hung Sin Nui once went to North Korea and Vietnam to perform. After 1980, her footsteps appeared in America, Canada, Singapore, Malaysia, Hong Kong and Macau. Every time she gave a Cantonese opera performance in a particular place, the popularity was unprecedented, and many people were attracted to see the performance (China Culture, 2010).

Liu (2013) pointed out in her news report that Hung Sin Nui's performance fascinated many people. She doesn't need to rehearse or be a director now. She hopes to train some actors and successors. When she cultivates fans in the theatre, she also cultivates audiences. How many audiences can a theatre fan bring out (see Figure 3.4)?

Renowned Performance Group – Yam Kim Fai and Pak Suet Sin

The next celebrities comprise one of the most famous Cantonese opera performance groups, Yam Kim Fai and Pak Suet Sin. In Hong Kong, almost everyone knows 'Yam & Pak' performance group even though someone is not a Cantonese opera fan (Guangzhou Digital Library, 2007). Many people were impressed not only by their performances on stage but also by their always-together relationship in real life. In the 1950s, the major entertainment and leisure activities of Hong Kong people included

Figure 3.4 Influences of Hung Sin Nui

Cantonese opera and film. At that time, Yam Kim Fai was already well-known for her excellent performance of Cantonese opera. Thus, many filmmakers realised the commercial value of her huge influence and invited her to participate in new films to attract audiences as much as possible. Yam Kim Fai has remarkably played the male leading actor in nearly 300 films. This setup deeply impressed many audiences for the vague boundary between her biological gender and stage gender. Most opera fans are female, covering all age groups and various social statuses (Guangzhou Digital Library, 2007). However, her partner Pak Suet Sin always presented herself as a very traditional female to audiences. This seamless and magic combination further enhances their performance and naturally wins the heart of fans. The last Cantonese opera film they co-acted is *Empress Li of the Southern Tang Dynasty*, which received 1.5 million HKD investment and took 2 years to produce. This film sets a record for the largest production, the longest screening period and the highest income of a Cantonese film (Guangzhou Digital Library, 2007). Lastly, *Jian Xue Fu Sheng* is a famous stage show produced based on the life story of Yam Kim Fai, Pak Suet Sin and Tang Ti Sheng Tang. Before the official release date, it had been fully booked for later 100 show times (Guangzhou Digital Library, 2007). This kind of data can further justify the massive influence of Yam & Pak group at that time.

To sum up, some Cantonese opera stars have a considerable influence regardless of whether it was during or after their careers, helping them receive a solid audience foundation. Most of them performed in various places, attracting a large number of audiences at that time. This kind of phenomenon is like star-chasing activities in modern societies (see Figure 3.5).

Influences of Modern Cantonese Opera Star Zeng Xiao Min

Lastly, a young but famous star, Zeng Xiao Min, is worth mentioning when looking at some Cantonese opera stars in modern times. Zeng Xiao Min is a national first-class actress who received the Shanghai Magnolia Theatre Award for The Best Lead Role Performer and Plum Blossom Award. She is the current dean of Guangdong Cantonese Theatre. In *Madame White Snake*, Zeng Xiao Min, who portrayed Bai Suzhen, presents her clear and sweet singing voice and delicate and elegant figure. She was appointed to be the dean of Guangdong Cantonese Opera Theatre in 2019. In recent years, the Guangdong Cantonese Opera Theatre has made the Cantonese Opera on Campus vivid and colourful. Last year, the theatre intended to cover fully the universities in Guangdong and expected to cover others in the future. She also intended to 'establish a senior lecturer group, giving lectures and performances in schools around the country, and opening a variety

Figure 3.5 Renowned Performance Group – Yam Kim Fai & Pak Suet Sin

of projects such as Cantonese Opera experience halls, allowing students to interact in the experience and enhancing the fun of the activities'.

Cantonese Opera on Campus invites famous Cantonese opera artists from Hong Kong and Macau to give lectures in the Mainland. This event also goes out of Guangdong. For example, in October 2019, the theatre went to three universities in Macau to perform related Cantonese opera popularisation activities. At the same time, Zeng Xiao Min aimed at the white-collar market and succeeded in creating brand projects, such as New Year's Show, Weekend Watch and Famous Performance Week, based on the principle of not sending one ticket. Market cultivation and box office revenue were also explored. These projects were considered successful. She firmly believes that the creative power and brand of Cantonese opera must not be lost, and the market for young people must be explored to allow the inheritance and development of Cantonese opera to continue (South China, 2019; Xinhua News, 2016). As a dean of Guangdong Cantonese opera theatre, Zeng Xiao Min led her team to develop various online Cantonese opera programmes and give performances online during the COVID-19 pandemic in 2020. An online concert, called Yueyun Online, received more than 5 million audience globally (China News, 2020b).

Figure 3.6 Influences of Modern Cantonese Opera Star Zeng Xiao Min

3.3.3 Cantonese Opera Heritage Museum

A museum is widely understood as a place to represent and preserve tangible cultural assets.

Hong Kong Heritage Museum – Cantonese Opera Heritage Hall

The visitors of the Hong Kong Heritage Museum show various interests; thus, the museum decides to present a unique mix of history, art and culture (Hong Kong Heritage Museum, 2020). On the one hand, the museum has a permanent gallery, Cantonese Opera Heritage Hall. This museum attraction presents more than 200 exhibits about the history and features of Cantonese opera. These exhibits include newspaper clippings about Cantonese opera and various costumes and documents. On the other hand, the museum also provides some thematic exhibitions, such as Virtuosity and Innovation – The Masterful Legacy of Lam Kar Sing and Splendour of Cantonese Opera:

Masters Tong Ti Sang and Yam Kim Fai. Since Hong Kong possesses a unique historical background and is historically a place that connects China and the world, the Hong Kong government wants to use heritage tourism and cultural tourism to increase the attractiveness and uniqueness of Hong Kong as a tourist destination. Li and Lo (2004) suggested the usage of cultural and historical resources on tourism. Therefore, Cantonese opera can also be a part of tourism resources not only for tourist consumption but also for city tourism branding by holding a permanent exhibition and designing related activities in heritage museums (see Figure 3.7).

The Art Museum of Cantonese Opera – Guangzhou

The Art Museum of Cantonese Opera is an essential cultural heritage in Lingnan (Guo & Li, 2015). One of museum's purposes is to provide an inheritance atmosphere for Cantonese opera; to serve this purpose, the museum preserves the spirit of Lingnan culture through acceptance and respect to other cultural spirits. This museum is more than just an exhibition centre or a place to study and perform Cantonese opera. It is a cultural space that connects the predecessors and the successors. Cantonese opera cannot

Figure 3.7 Hong Kong Heritage Museum

be preserved, inherited or developed unless it is embedded in the daily lives of the public (Guo & Li, 2015).

Similar to the spirit of Lingnan culture, Cantonese opera demonstrates worldliness and open and innovative art with an economical and pragmatic nature. The stage, singing and costumes of Cantonese opera are closely related to people's everyday lives, that is, the fundamental principle of the design of the Art Museum of Cantonese Opera (Guo & Li, 2015). The design of the museum is in line with the traditional spirit. It incorporates the continuation and public nature of contemporary life. For example, the main hall is designed with a public corridor where the former citizen market pathway is maintained on the site, thereby making an open walkway with a close connection with the urban roads. People can simultaneously enjoy both the traditional garden and the urban public space. In addition, this design can integrate memories with modern days. As a result, the Art Museum of Cantonese Opera becomes an integral place full of historical memory and contemporary life (Guo & Li, 2015).

Macau Museum

Macau is a city which highly advocates multi-culture and diversity. Many people in Macau are mainly from Guangdong and Fujian. Thus, Macau offers abundant local entertainment and regional characteristics. Cantonese opera, which is amongst the most popular entertainment activities, has influenced Macau residents for many generations (Macau Museum, 2016).

Cantonese opera is embedded into Macau culture. Thus, the Macau Museum has held permanent Cantonese opera exhibitions to present historical and cultural value further through various objects. In addition to permanent exhibits, various thematic activities in the forms of exhibitions, lectures and workshops (e.g., Masterpieces of Human Intangible Cultural Heritage – Cantonese Opera Photographs Exhibition, The Enchanting Red Boat – An Episode of the Cantonese Opera Culture, a thematic talk titled The Enchanting Red Boat, a workshop by the Macau Lai Chon Chinese Opera Association) are also related to Cantonese opera (Macau Museum, 2016) (see Figure 3.8).

Cantonese Star Former Residences

Tangible buildings, including heritage museums and cultural attractions, can present intangible history and cultural values and be packaged for tourist consumption. Therefore, the former residences of Cantonese opera stars, which can serve as tourism attractions, have the potential to present intangible cultural values and memories of the traditional performing arts.

Figure 3.8 Macau Museum

Guangzhou, as a hub of Cantonese culture, is a home for many Cantonese opera stars. Enning Road, near the famous Shangxiajiu Pedestrian Shopping Street, has a history of 100 years and spans 1,500 meters in downtown Guangzhou. It features more than ten cultural and historical relics. The following table presents the basic information about some Cantonese opera stars' former residences in Guangzhou (see Table 3.1).

Table 3.1 shows that many Cantonese opera stars have their former residences in Guangzhou. Most of their residences have been listed as Protected Cultural Relics of Liwan District, Guangzhou. In 2012, when the Guangzhou Cantonese Art Museum was still at the stage of site selection, Chen Jianhua, mayor of Guangzhou at that time, proposed an idea to integrate the heritage museum into the rejuvenation programme of Enning Road, making the whole area become a place for promoting and displaying Cantonese opera and Lingnan culture and eventually increasing both the cultural and social value of the Xiguan district (Sina Finance, 2019). In 2009, Professor Li Yizhuang wrote a letter to Zhu Xiaodan, the secretary of the Guangzhou Municipal Committee at that time. The professor pointed out that the Cantonese opera stars' former residence cluster in Enning Road, comprising non-renewable relics, is truly the most remarkable historical cultural heritage in Guangzhou. Professor Li Yizhuang expressed his hope to preserve and inherit this residence cluster, trying to make good use of its

Table 3.1 Cantonese Opera Stars' Residences in Guangzhou

Name of Stars	Location of the former residence	Additional information
Cheung Wood Yau	No. 23 Shiliufu Alley, Baohua Road, Liwan District, Guangzhou City.	Chung Wood Yau began his career in 1936 as a principal actor in both civil and martial roles in Cantonese Opera. But it was in Hong Kong three years later, in the film 'Breaking through the Bronze Net' (1939), that he made his big screen debut. His career peaked between 1949 and 1952 when he averaged an output of 20-plus films a year, including the two-part blockbuster 'Crime Doesn't Pay – Part two' (1949). Cheung began appearing in television dramas on TVB from 1972 and retired in 1982. His former residence was listed as 'Liwan District Protected Historical Site'
Lee Hoi Chuen	No. 13 Yongqing Alley, Enning Road, Liwan District, Guangzho City.	As a famous clown, he became famous in the 1930s for acting in 'Robbing the dead'. Liao Xiahuai; Ban Ri An; Ye Foruo and he were called 'Top Four Clowns in Cantonese Opera'. His main plays include *Alms for the Scholar*. His former residence was listed as 'Liwan District Protected Historical Site'
Couple Shao-Jia Liang & Jun-Yu Lang	No. 29 Changhua Street, Liwan District, Guangzhou City.	**Shao-Jia Liang:** As a famous sub-martial role, he was titled 'Leading Martial Scholar of the Times'. His main plays included *Meeting by the West River, Three Marshals Besieged on Mount Yao, Ten Impeachment of Yim Sung and Chew Chi Lung Fights to Cross the River*. **Jun-Yu Lang:** As a famous young female character type. She is good at both civil and military performance and both young male and female character types. In terms of aria, her true voice was of broad diapason, which enabled her to sing in either low or loud voice freely; her falsetto was either firm or gentle with lasting appeal. Her main plays included *The Lady General and Memorial at the Pagoda*. Former residence was listed as 'Liwan District Protected Historical Site'
Couple Ma Sze Tsang & Hung Sin Nui	No. 20 Youai Road, Huaqiao Village, Yuexiu District, Guangzhou City.	**Hung Sin Nui:** As a famous young female character type, she created the 'Nu Qiang' when starring in Yi Dai Tian Jiao. In 1952, she organised to set up Chun Sin Mei Opera Troupe and acted in *Princess Zhaojun*. This is also when she modified the 'Nu Qiang' into the 'Hong Qiang'. Both types of singing are famous at home and abroad. In 1957, she went to the Soviet Union to medal for her singing of *Princess Zhaojun*. From then on, she created a lot of art images on the stage successfully. In 1998, the Guangzhou Municipal People's Government founded the 'Hung Sin Nui Art Centre' to exhibit and study her creations and artistic achievements. In 2002, the Ministry of Culture granted her the first 'Presentation & Performance Art Creation and Research Achievements Prize'. Her main plays included *Searching the Academy; Guan Hanqing, Shanxiang Fengyun and Princess Zhaojun*.

priceless cultural value and hopefully make it a distinguished 'identity card' of Guangzhou City (Sina Finance, 2019).

Other Tangible Buildings

In Hong Kong, some places, apart from heritage museums, are recommended for tourists to experience Cantonese opera culture and have a memorable experience. Firstly, Xiqu Centre in West Kowloon Cultural District is an excellent place for amateurs and beginners (HKTB, 2021). Similar to the main purpose of other Cantonese opera theatres, such as Yau Ma Tei Theatre and Ko Shan Theatre New Wing, the centre's primary purpose is opera performances. Secondly, Sunbeam Theatre is an ideal choice for those tourists who seek the ultimate local Cantonese opera experience. Sunbeam Theatre opened in 1972. It has been a major attraction ever since. Not many places in Hong Kong held shows almost every evening. Despite the rumours that the theatre will shut down because of the decrease in sales, the theatre continues to attract regular customers. Moreover, many Cantonese opera performers' dreams include holding a show in Sunbeam Theatre.

In Macau, two theatres are listed on the website of the Macao Government Tourism Office (MGTO). The first is Cheng Peng Theatre. The theatre is located on a narrow street off the main Avenida de Almeida Ribeiro, which was once part of the wetland at the Inner Harbour. The theatre was built in 1875 and presented Cantonese opera to the local audience. The theatre started showing films as well later. However, it was closed down in 1992 along with the declining theatre industry in the 1990s. It was turned into a warehouse for storage purposes and was abandoned after. At present, tourists can still see the fading Chinese characters of its name carved on its exterior wall as a record for visitors to trace back its history (MGTO, 2021a).

The second is Alegria Cinema. The more than 60-year-old Alegria Cinema is located at the intersection of Travessa da Corda and Estrada do Repouso of the San Kio area, a densely populated and historical district of Macau. It was built under the initiative of a group of Chinese merchants headed by Ho Yin, an eminent social figure of the past. Besides movie screening, the cinema was equipped with a large stage in 1957 to turn it into a major venue for community activities and Cantonese opera performances in Macau. Famed Cantonese opera troupes of Hong Kong, like Chor Fung Ming Opera Troupe, and reputable opera artists, like Lam Kar Sing, graced the cinema stage. The local singing associations are its regular users, and community activities of different natures are held (MGTO, 2021b).

In brief, if they could be well developed, these kinds of tangible buildings can serve as valuable tourism resources not only for culture inheritance and promotion but also for diverse tourist experience. As one of the most representative traditional cultures in the GBA, Cantonese opera evidently requires much attention from the government, academia and industry to be developed and rejuvenated as a distinguished tourism resource in both tangible and intangible dimensions.

3.4 Summary

In short, as the three major cities in the GBA, Hong Kong, Macau and Guangzhou, actively integrate Cantonese opera into various festivals to make people appreciate this priceless intangible cultural heritage, enriching the residents' leisure activities. In addition, this integration is an effective way to inherit and rejuvenate Cantonese opera as one of the most representative Lingnan culture that has been inscribed on the UNESCO's Representative List of the Intangible Cultural Heritage of Humanity in 2009. Lastly, Cantonese opera has gradually become an attractive tourism resource in terms of tourism development. This resource has huge potential to serve as one of the new directions of future tourism development in the GBA and a unique selling point of tourism products if this resource is appropriately utilised. However, various cooperation amongst different stakeholders (e.g., government, industry and academic) should be largely encouraged to explore and utilise the value of Cantonese opera.

Along with the successful development of Cantonese opera, some famous Cantonese opera stars in the three major cities in the GBA, Hong Kong, Macau and Guangzhou, are briefly introduced in the preceding paragraphs. Their influences are unquestionably significant. From attracting a large number of visitors by delivering various kinds of performances in both domestic and overseas to promoting Cantonese opera amongst the young people by bringing the performance into schools, these so-called celebrity influences shall be properly used to develop and rejuvenate further the valuable Cantonese opera culture, with the hope that it can serve as a new tourism resource in the GBA in the future.

References

Ahmad, Y. (2006). The Scope and Definitions of Heritage: From Tangible to Intangible. *International Journal of Heritage Studies*, 12(3), 292–300.

Carnegie, E., & McCabe, S. (2008). Re-Enactment Events and Tourism: Meaning, Authenticity and Identity. *Current Issues in Tourism*, 11(4), 349–367. doi:10.1080/13683500802140380.

Chhabra, D. (2010). Branding Authenticity. *Tourism Analysis*, 15(6), 735–740. doi: 10.3727/108354210X12904412050134.

China Culture. (2010). *Celebrity Hung Sin-niu*. Retrieved February 16, 2021, from http://en.chinaculture.org/gb/2010-04/09/content_375842.htm.

China News. (2020a, May 28). Traditional *Culture "Spokesperson"* Zeng Xiaomin: Young *People Are* the *Most Real Future* of *Opera Art*. Retrieved March 16, 2021, from www.chinanews.com/gn/2020/05-28/9196992.shtml.

China News. (2020b, May 30). *Introducing Cantonese Opera Elements into the Park Guangzhou Yuexiu Park Becomes the First Case in Guangdong*. Retrieved March 16, 2021, from www.chinanews.com/cul/2020/05-30/9199030.shtml.

Connell, J., & Gibson, C. (2004). World Music: Deterritorializing Place and Identity. *Progress in Human Geography*, 28(3), 342–361.

Cultural Heritage of Macau. (n.d.). *Tam Kong Festival*. Retrieved February 16, 2021, from www.culturalheritage.mo/cn/detail/2776/1.

De Rojas, C., & Camarero, C. (2008). Visitors' Experience, Mood and Satisfaction in a Heritage Context: Evidence from an Interpretation Center. *Tourism Management*, 29(3), 525–537.

Diettrich, B. (2015). Performing Arts as Cultural Heritage in the Federated States of Micronesia. *International Journal of Heritage Studies*, 21(7), 660–673.

Du Cros, H. (2007). Too Much of a Good Thing? Visitor Congestion Management Issues for Popular World Heritage Tourist Attractions. *Journal of Heritage Tourism*, 2(3), 225–237. doi:10.2167/ jht062.0.

Fremaux, S., & Fremaux, M. (2013). Remembering the Beatles'legacy in Hamburg's Problematic Tourism Strategy. *Journal of Heritage Tourism*, 8(4), 303–319. doi:10.1080/ 1743873X.2013.799172.

Gapinski, J. (1988). Tourism's Contribution to the Demand for London's Lively Arts. *Applied Economics*, 20(7), 957–968. doi:10.1080/00036848800000019.

Gilmore, A., Carson, D., & Ascenc ̃ao, M. (2007). Sustainable Tourism Marketing at a World Heritage Site. *Journal of Strategic Marketing*, 15(2–3), 253–264. doi:10.1080/09652540701318930.

Guangzhou Digital Library. (2007, September 11). *Cantonese Opera Stars: Yam & Pak. Inside and Outside the Hu-Du-Men, They Are Always Classical Partner*. Retrieved March 16, 2021, from www.gzlib.org.cn/gzrw/151582.jhtml.

Guo, Q., & Li, X. (2015). Integrated Conservation of the Cantonese Opera Art Museum and Intangible Cultural Heritage. *The International Archives of Photogrammetry, Remote Sensing and Spatial Information Sciences*, 40(5), 187.

Hede, A.-M. (2008). World Heritage Listing and the Evolving Issues Related to Tourism and Heritage: Cases from Australia and New Zealand. *Journal of Heritage Tourism*, 2(3), 133–143. doi:10.2167/jht055.0.

Henke, L. L. (2005). Music Induced Tourism: Strategic Use of Indigenous Music as a Tourist Icon. *Journal of Hospitality & Leisure Marketing*, 13(2), 3–18.

Hong Kong Heritage Museum. (2020, December). *The Museum*. Retrieved March 16, 2021, from https://hk.heritage.museum/en_US/web/hm/aboutus/themuseum.html.

Hong Kong Tourism Board (HKTB). (2021). *7 Places to Discover Cantonese Opera in Hong Kong*. Retrieved March 16, 2021, from www.discoverhongkong.com/ eng/explore/arts/discover-cantonese-opera-in-hong-kong.html.

ICOMOS. (2002). *International Cultural Tourism Charter*. Principles and Guidelines Formanaging Tourism at Places of Cultural and Heritage Significance. ICOMOS Inter-National Cultural Tourism Committee.

Io, M. U. (2018). Collaboration Between Practitioners and Public Agencies in Preserving and Promoting Musical Heritage in Macao. *Journal of Heritage Tourism*, 1–14.

Li, Y., & Lo, R. L. B. (2004). Applicability of the market appeal—robusticity matrix: a case study of heritage tourism. *Tourism Management,* 25(6), 789–800.

Littrell, M. A., & Miller, N. J. (2001). Marketing Across Cultures: Consumers' Perception of Product Complexity, Familiarity, and Compatibility. *Journal of Global Marketing,* 15(1), 67–86.

Liu, Q. (2013, May 17). *Hung Sin-niu: Never Stop the Pace of Exploration and Innovation in Cantonese Opera.* Retrieved March 16, 2021, from http://cn.cccweb.org/portal/pubinfo/2020/04/28/200001004002/98856a86e8db4d1e9076b8e903950d99.html#.

Lo, W. H. (2015). The Music Culture of Older Adults in Cantonese Operatic Singing Lessons. *Ageing and Society,* 35(8), 1614–1634.

Lo, W. H. (2017). Traditional Opera and Young People: Cantonese Opera as Personal Development. *International Journal of Adolescence and Youth,* 22(2), 238–249.

Macao Government Tourism Office (MGTO). (2021a). *Yueju Opera (Cantonese Opera).* Retrieved March 16, 2021, from www.macaotourism.gov.mo/en/shows-and-entertainment/shows/yueju-opera-cantonese-opera.

Macao Government Tourism Office (MGTO). (2021b). *Cheng Peng Theatre.* Retrieved March 16, 2021, from www.macaotourism.gov.mo/en/suggested-tours/footsteps-into-the-historic-centre/cheng-peng-theatre.

Macau Cultural Affairs Bureau. (2016). *Exhibition "The Enchanting Red Boat" at the Macau Museum Is Extended.* Retrieved March 16, 2021, from www.icm.gov.mo/en/news/detail/14168.

Macau Museum. (2016, May). *The Enchanting Red Boat – An Episode of the Cantonese Opera Culture.* Retrieved March 16, 2021, from www.macaumuseum.gov.mo/w3eng/w3MMexhibition/tempExhi_redBoat.aspx.

Macau Travel Talk. (2019, May). *30th Macao Arts Festival Turns the Spotlight on Traditional Classics.* Retrieved March 16, 2021, from https://mtt.macaotourism.gov.mo/201905/en/contents/2/1088.html.

Mason, K. (2004). Sound and Meaning in Aboriginal Tourism. *Annals of Tourism Research,* 31(4), 837–854. doi:10.1016/j.annals.2004.03.006.

Miichi, K. (2016). Playful Relief Folk Performing Arts in Japan After the 2011 Tsunami. *Asian Ethnology,* 75(1), 139–162.

Park, H. (2011). Shared National Memory as Intangible Heritage: Re-Imagining Two Koreas as One Nation. *Annals of Tourism Research,* 38(2), 520–539.

Poria, Y., Reichel, A., & Biran, A. (2006). Heritage Site Perceptions and Motivations to Visit. *Journal of Travel Research,* 44(3), 318–326.

Richards, G. (1996). *Cultural Tourism in Europe.* Wallingford: CABI Publications.

Sina Finance. (2019, April 26). *10 Famous Cantonese Opera Actors' Former Residences Are in the Enning Road Reconstruction Zone, Calling for Protection, and Linking Up the Cantonese Opera Cultural Belt with the Museum and Behe Artist Association (1).* Retrieved March 16, 2021, from https://finance.sina.com.cn/roll/2019-04-26/doc-ihvhiqax5102817.shtml.

South China. (2019, September 12). *Zeng Xiaoming Appointed as the Dean of Guangdong Cantonese Opera Theatre.* Retrieved March 16, 2021, from http://news.cctv.com/2019/09/12/ARTIeGFrY6gaIzzaTPc9BFs1190912.shtml.

Tikkanen, I. (2008). Internationalization Process of a Music Festival: Case Kuhmo Chamber Music Festival. *Journal of Euromarketing,* 17(2), 127–139.

UNESCO. (2001). *UNESCO Universal Declaration on Cultural Diversity.* Retrieved March 11, 2021, from http://portal.unesco.org/en/ev.php-URL_ ID=13179&URL_DO=DO_TOPIC&URL_SECTION=201.html.

UNESCO. (2003a). *Text of the Convention for the Safeguarding of the Intangible Cultural Heritage.* Retrieved March 16, 2021, from www.unesco.org/culture/ich/ en/convention#art2.

UNESCO. (2003b). *What Is Intangible Cultural Heritage – Definitions of Article 2 in the Text of Convention.* Retrieved March 16, 2021, from https://ich.unesco.org/ en/performing-arts-00054.

UNESCO. (2009). *Yueju Opera.* Retrieved March 16, 2021, from https://ich.unesco. org/en/RL/yueju-opera-00203.

Van der Hoeven, A. (2012). The Popular Music Heritage of the Dutch Pirates: Illegal Radio and Cultural Identity. *Media, Culture & Society*, 34(8), 927–943.

The Venetian Macau. (2020, November). *1st Guangdong-Hong Kong-Macao Greater Bay Area Chinese Opera Cultural Festival.* Retrieved March 16, 2021, from www.venetianmacao.com/entertainment/chinese-opera-cultural-festival.html?_ ga=2.106034755.1135979524.1608960643-1907591199.1608442703.

Xie, P. F., & Lane, B. (2006). A Life Cycle Model for Aboriginal Arts Performance in Tourism: Perspectives on Authenticity. *Journal of Sustainable Tourism*, 14(6), 545–561. doi:10.2167/jost 601.0.

Xie, P. F., Osumare, H., & Ibrahim, A. (2007). Gazing the Hood: Hip-Hop as Tourism Attraction. *Tourism Management*, 28(2), 452–460. doi:10.1016/j.tourman. 2006.03.009.

Xinhua News. (2016). *Cultural Celebrities in Guangdong.* Retrieved March 16, 2021, from www.gd.xinhuanet.com/gdstatics/mrkgd/zxm/?from=singlemessage.

Xinhua News. (2020, November 26). *The 8th Yangcheng Cantonese Opera Festival Ended Successfully.* Retrieved March 16, 2021, from http://m.xinhuanet.com/ gd/2020-11/26/c_1126787192.htm.

4 Cantonese Opera and Cultural Heritage Tourism in the Greater Bay Area

4.1 Cultural Heritage Tourism

Many scholars (McKercher & Du Cros, 2002; Timothy & Boyd, 2003) claim that cultural heritage tourism is a significant and rapidly growing section of tourism. The history of cultural heritage tourism can be dated back to ancient times (Timothy & Boyd, 2003). Many ancient travel records were collected by explorers, sailors, traders and adventurers. Cultural heritage tourism has recently attracted millions of tourists every year (Timothy & Boyd, 2006). More than 40% of world tourism is related to cultural heritage tourism, and it is expected to grow at 15% every year (Timothy & Boyd, 2003). One of the reasons is the world heritage list. When the list was introduced in the last century, people became much more aware of the heritage sites and attractions in the world. The demand and supply of related tourism products increased dramatically. However, the precise definition of cultural heritage tourism is missing. The general understanding of this term includes a group or subgroup of tourists interested in human heritage, such as historical buildings or beautiful attractions. Timothy and Boyd (2003) classified heritage tourism into natural heritage tourism, cultural heritage tourism and urban heritage tourism. However, these categories are not mutually exclusive; hence, they overlap with many other forms of tourism.

Cultural heritage tourism is not only a type of tourism but also an investment that can improve people's lives and society. On the one hand, culture is a catalyst to the development of new products and services. In addition, tourism is related to many other sectors. The increase of tourists brings revenue and profit, which is beneficial to economic growth. On the other hand, the development of cultural heritage tourism also raises the destination's attention to manage and preserve their cultural heritage (Di Pietro et al., 2015). Cultural heritage not only includes the attractions or sites but also their customs and traditions. Therefore, different stakeholders must

DOI: 10.4324/9781003157564-4

cooperate with one another to sustain cultural heritage tourism (International Council on Monuments and Sites, 1998).

Traditional performing arts belong to intangible cultural heritage. Therefore, they share many similar experiential attributes, such as authenticity and learning experience, with tangible cultural heritage. These experiential attributes are usually the reasons why people visit historical sites and attend cultural events (Io, 2019). Some scholars (Xie & Lane, 2006) claim that tourists can easily understand the culture, history and custom of a destination via performing arts, such as music, dance or ritual. In addition, the development of performing arts also leads to the development of musical theatres and other infrastructures for performance. The modern explosion in art performances for visitors is multifaceted in the cause, ranging from supply factors (e.g., heritage planning, economic need and cultural revival) to demand factors (e.g., the desire for creative, authentic experiences and entertainment by and for visitors) (Apostolakis, 2003).

In Cantonese opera, its intrinsic craftsmanship refers to its inner artistic components, such as its music and acting style, stage costume and makeup (Macau Cultural Affairs Bureau, 2016). Cantonese opera shows its intrinsic characteristics in its vibrant performance style combining dance, drama, martial arts, music, singing and verse, colourful costumes, makeup and intricate gestures (Macau Cultural Affairs Bureau, 2016). All these intrinsic components shape the performing style of Cantonese opera and differentiate it from other genres of performing arts (UNESCO, 2009). Like the other genres of performing arts heritage, Cantonese opera's craftsmanship may require time for the foreigners to appreciate and enjoy it fully.

4.2 Cultural Heritage Tourism in the Greater Bay Area (GBA)

4.2.1 Hong Kong Cantonese Opera Culture Tour

In Hong Kong, many attractions or sites are recognised as a national or international heritage. Many of these attractions or sites are heritage in postcolonial contexts with simultaneous remembering, forgetting and reimagining (Yeoh, 2001). After Hong Kong returned to China in 1997, localisation became very popular. Localisation takes many different forms, and cultural heritage is one of them (Barber, 2019). These cultural heritages, such as buildings, markets, shops and other landscape features, are the collective memories of many Hong Kong people (Henderson, 2008). In addition to these monumental types of heritage, non-monumental heritage also becomes increasingly popular to both locals and tourists. One non-monumental heritage is the cultural heritage walking tours. This tour started around 20 years ago. Hong Kong is a very popular tourist destination. It is famous for its shopping and dining experiences and is recognised as the hub of Asia for many tourists. After the Asian Financial Crisis in 1997, the Hong Kong government began to realise the vulnerability of tourism. Hence, the government started to explore other options for tourism. Cultural tourism, as well as heritage tourism, was considered one of their directions (McKercher et al., 2005). The change of this direction, combined with the opening of the Individual Visit Scheme in 2003, made Hong Kong the most frequently visited city in the world. Most tourists come to Hong Kong to enjoy the shopping and dining experiences, and their attentions are seldom on Hong Kong's cultural heritage. However, the introduction of cultural heritage tourism offers tourists other options to explore Hong Kong, presenting another growth focus for tourism in Hong Kong.

Many Chinese opera performances have been held in Hong Kong during the Chinese Opera Festival since 2010. Many renowned stars from Kunqu, Peking opera and Cantonese opera come to Hong Kong to perform. The visitors are exposed to various selections. They can enjoy the show and learn the characteristics of different operas in China. In addition to opera performances, the festival also invites experts and performers to provide seminars to share their experiences and insights. The festival offers an excellent opportunity to demonstrate China's soft power and its development.

In addition to the Chinese Opera Festival, the Hong Kong Tourism Board initiated the Hong Kong Cantonese Opera Culture Tour in 2013 (HKTB, 2021). As the tour name suggests, this tour allows participants to explore Cantonese opera, a traditional art form famed for its colourful costumes, distinctive singing and intricate symbolic movement. In this fascinating tour of Chinese arts, people can also explore Xiqu theatres and a qipao shop where they can get to make their own souvenirs. Tourists get hands-on experience of Chinese arts and crafts, learn the history of qipao and explore old streets and the oldest public housing complex in the city to discover Hong Kong's past. The tour itinerary includes the following: (1) visiting the heritage of Mei Ho House museum and Apliu Street, (2) wandering around Sham Shui Po, (3) joining a DIY bookmark workshop in a qipao shop, (4) visiting the Ko Shan Theatre Education Centre, (5) enjoying a seafood dinner and (6) visiting the Western Kowloon Cultural District – Xiqu Centre (see Figure 4.1).

4.2.2 Macau's Cultural Cards

Macau was a Portuguese colony before it returned to China's sovereignty in 1999. It was originally a port for international trade in China. Macau has been a Portuguese colony for a long period; thus, it has inherited various features from Western culture, and these cultural elements are embedded

Figure 4.1 Western Kowloon Cultural District – Xiqu Centre (Hong Kong)

in many people's daily lives (Vong, 2013). Luo and Lam (2016) claim that Macau is a 'melting pot of East and West', which is, in their own words, 'an exotic flower in the blossoming garden of diverse Chinese Architecture'. Clayton (2013) claims Macau is a 'city of museums' to demonstrate how abundant Macau's cultural resources are. The Macau government, as well as its citizens, value these cultural and heritage resources highly. These cultural and heritage resources contain important cultural meanings and distinct characteristics, showing that Macau possesses abundant intangible and tangible cultural and heritage resources. For example, the Historic Centre of Macau has many residential, religious and public historical buildings. The buildings' architecture reflects the influence of both Portugal and China in terms of aesthetics, culture, religion and technology. Macau is an important port for international trade in China. Thus, many people, especially merchants, settled in Macau. These merchants, as well as their families, bring not only wealth to Macau but also their religion and culture, which can be seen via different building types. Many of these buildings are still in use. These buildings adapt the design of Chinese and West simultaneously, such as incorporating Chinese-type ornaments on the baroque-mannerist church façade of St. Paul's Ruins, the separation between the seascape and property of a typical port city and the blending of urban fabric infrastructure into narrow and long streets. The intangible influence of Western cultures can also be found in the daily lives of people in Macau, such as religion, education, language and food. Discussing the individual quality of each historical site is not meaningful because the value is reflected not only in the buildings and the customs of the people but also in a mixture of all.

Macau has been developing rapidly during recent decades. Land reclamation began in the 19th century to resolve the problem of limited land. This action changed the coastline, but the historical centre remains intact. The historical centre continues to connect with the sea, Guia Lighthouse, the Outer Harbour, A-Ma Temple, the Mount Fortress and the Penha Hills. Since 2005, new development pressures have existed outside the limits of the property. These pressures have encouraged the expansion of detailed planning control guidelines beyond the limits of the inscribed site, with a special focus on retaining visual corridors between the historic centre and the seascape and towards the riverside. The type, design and materials used by many historical sites in Macau demonstrate the value of these buildings. Many of these buildings retain their original function nowadays. The public square, which remains its original function, is associated with many local traditions, such as worship and processions. The rapid development of Macau, along with the fact that many of these buildings are located near the trading port, can easily damage the authenticity of these buildings, especially the critical visual links to the Outer Harbour and the river.

In the last 400 years, Macau was the place that connects the West and China. Macau contains some of the oldest and best-preserved Western-style buildings, from Baroque to neoclassical. Many religious buildings have different religious features. The design of these buildings combined different cultures. For example, some buildings incorporated the Chinese and Indian culture by painting the Guia Chapel in Chinese style. The building styles and architecture in the Historic Centre of Macau are very diverse.

Cantonese opera in Macau had a rapid development in the 20th century. Famous Cantonese opera stars, such as Yam Kim Fai and Pak Suet Sin, regularly performed in Macau. Zhang (2010) claims that Cantonese opera was the most popular genre in the 20th century. Although the popularity of Cantonese opera in the last few years has decreased, the fan base and the number of performing troupes remain large (Io, 2019). Regular performances of Cantonese opera are held in Macau, and Cantonese opera is frequently performed on TV, radio and some local festivals in Macau. For example, Estabelecimento de Comidas Tai Long Fong, a classic restaurant that serves you feasts for mouth and ears, has more than70 years of history (see Figure 4.2). It is the only Cantonese opera tea house remaining in Macau, as

Figure 4.2 Estabelecimento de Comidas Tai Long Fong Restaurant (Macau)

its owner, Ms. Chan, is committed to preserving the culture of Cantonese operatic singing in Macau. The recipes of its dim sum, such as lotus seed paste puff and jumbo steamed chicken bun, have remained unchanged for decades. Thus, you taste not just a fine dim sum at Tai Long Fong but also a piece of Macau's fading history. This restaurant calms your heart with a treat on your taste buds and ears. Whether you are in love or lovelorn or whether you succeeded or failed yesterday is not important at this moment. Looking at your today's self from a distant past like a time traveller, you will suddenly realise that every emotion in life is nothing longer than a song or heavier than a wisp of smoke.

4.2.3 Guangdong's Traditional Features

Intangible cultural heritage became very popular in Chinese society with the launching day of Cultural Heritage in 2006 (Zhang, 2017). In recent years, much attention has been paid to the tourism development of intangible cultural heritage. Museum, theme park and the real-life scenery stage are often regarded as the three most common methods to turn intangible cultural resources into tourism products. The museum of intangible cultural heritage mainly presents heritage in a static state and protects the authenticity of intangible cultural heritage. The theme park of intangible cultural heritage rebuilds the authenticity of intangible cultural heritage and virtualises the experience space, achieving the materialisation of the heritage landscape. The real-life scenery stage, the most traditional method, is based on people's performing activities. Many cultural products in Guangdong continue to adopt the traditional techniques, from production to marketing and sales. These products do not evolve according to customers' needs. Furthermore, many of these products do not precisely reflect and explore the traditional and cultural meanings. Hence, one should reconsider and redesign these products from the functional, aesthetic and philosophical levels to increase the emotional connection with customers.

The following are the three main clans of Guangdong traditions: Guangfu, Hakka and Chaoshan. The rich and diverse cultural resources allow Guangdong to become one of the most frequently visited destinations for cultural tourists. Lingnan culture is a result of the mixture of Chinese culture. It is an inseparable part of Chinese culture. It is a culture based on local farming and fishing experience and integrated with foreign culture. Therefore, Lingnan culture is an open, pragmatic and creative culture with substantial adaptive potential.

Based on the geographical location, the three classifications of Lingnan culture include Guangdong, Guangxi and Hainan culture. The history of Guangzhou, which is also one of the centres of Chinese culture, can be traced back to the Neolithic period. In the history of China, Guangdong was usually the place that connected with different cultures. Hence, Cantonese culture is famous for its ability to accommodate many different cultures. This characteristic can be easily found in the architecture, customs, gardening, business and religion of many archaeological relics and historic sites, languages, music, operas, calligraphy, painting, poems and handicraft in people's daily lives.

At present, Cantonese opera represents the tradition of the Guangdong region and reflects the cultural, cosmological and religious aspects of Cantonese people. Cantonese operas are performed during religious festivals as well as at public and private social gatherings. In Guangzhou, musicians and singers can practice Cantonese opera by joining interest groups or professional troupes, depending on the experiences and levels of the musicians. The city offers different platforms for musicians to gather and perform. Cantonese opera performances took place in numerous venues, from public parks to newly built state-appointed theatres. People could also enjoy Cantonese opera performances every afternoon in certain restaurants or tea houses. Musicians also often gathered around associations or private apartments to practice (Cheung, 2019).

For example, Guangzhou is the hub for intangible cultural heritage in the GBA Tour (Guangzhou International, 2019). On 2 September 2019, more than 30 journalists from nine Southeast Asian Internet media groups and a dozen Chinese media groups at both central and provincial levels visited Guangzhou, a global city with a long and profound history, forming part of the Southeast Asian Media Greater Bay Area Tour. One of the destinations of the tour was Yong Qing Fang. Yong Qing Fong is home to the city's trademark arcade houses and possesses precious memories of Guangzhou as a commercial hub for 2,000 years. The area, established in 1931, is a well-known centre of Lingnan culture and Guangdong culture. Although this area is less than 8,000 square meters, people can find exhibition houses and a museum that showcases Canton porcelain, Canton embroidery and Cantonese opera, as well as Bruce Lee's ancestral home and many former residences of well-known figures. In recent years, the façades of the buildings located in Yong Qing Fang have been extensively renovated, but the original layout and special residences were preserved. Yong Qing Fang has since become a successful fusion of new and old in keeping with current trends.

The Cantonese Opera Art Museum located on Enning Road was the highlight of the tour. In the past, many famous Cantonese opera performers got together or lived in this neighbourhood. Many former residences of Cantonese opera performers, such as Ma Sze Tsang and Hung Sin Nui, are located near this area (see Figure 4.3). The saying, 'where there are Chinese people, you can hear Cantonese Opera', indicates how famous Cantonese opera

Figure 4.3 Yong Qing Fong (Guangzhou)

was before and at present overseas. A large number of Cantonese Chinese immigrated to Southeast Asia. Therefore, given that many Cantonese opera troupes and artists also went to the region, Southeast Asia is acclaimed as 'the second hometown of Cantonese Opera'.

In 2009, based on the joint application by Guangdong, Hong Kong and Macau, Cantonese opera was inscribed to the UNESCO's Representative List of the Intangible Cultural Heritage of Humanity. The Cantonese Opera Art Museum is committed to protecting, passing down and promoting the art of Cantonese opera. In addition, the Museum aims to share the essence and charm of Cantonese opera and Lingnan culture through exhibitions, performances, cultural exchanges and education. The Cantonese Opera Art Museum was built with many traditional Lingnan architectural features. It offers themed exhibitions, a theatre, garden and education spaces. It has attracted people from home and abroad, such as a delegation of mayors from the United States, Fortune Global Forum's global media group, the spouses of Fortune Global Forum guests and a delegation led by the former French Prime Minister Jean-Pierre Raffarin, to watch Cantonese opera performances. This museum continues to bring Cantonese opera to the global stage.

In the afternoon, the journalists visited the Exhibition Hall of Science Square and Guangzhou Leafun Culture Science and Technology Co., Ltd. to learn about how Guangzhou-based enterprises became leaders in the new forms of business based on cultural experiences. Leafun Culture Science and Technology Co., Ltd., established in 1997, specialises in culture and creative industries. With the philosophy of integrating culture with technology, it provides customers with innovative solutions and comprehensive technical support for artistic and cultural performances, cultural facility construction, culture and leisure tourism, cultural exhibitions and urban cultural landscapes based on its expertise in professional audio devices, lighting, video products and integrated control. At the Development Exhibition Hall for Science Square in Guangzhou Development District, the up-to-date technology products manufactured by Huangpu District attracted the journalists' attention. They were wowed by the VR and AR technology, drones, industrial robots and palm print recognition technology. After a few days, the journalists went to Dongguan, Shenzhen, Zhuhai and Zhongshan to understand the latest achievements in the development of the GBA (Guangzhou International, 2019).

4.3 Summary

Cantonese opera is a very popular performing art for many people, especially the elderly, in Hong Kong, Macau and Guangdong. It is also a piece of traditional music representing Cantonese culture and the collective memory of many people. Cantonese opera developed rapidly in the 20th century. However, its use as a tourism product was not fully explored and developed. One possible reason is that many tourists do not understand or have sufficient experience with Cantonese opera. GBA development allows the integration of intangible cultural heritages using Cantonese opera as a new method.

References

Apostolakis, A. (2003). The Convergence Process in Heritage Tourism. *Annals of Tourism Research*, 30(4), 795–812.

Barber, L. B. (2019). Heritage Tours and Trails on Foot in Hong Kong: Towards a Typology That Crosses the Tourist-Local Divide. *Journal of Heritage Tourism*, 14(4), 295–307.

Cheung, A. L. (2019). The Voices of the Voiceless: The Cantonese Opera Music Community in Guangzhou, China. *Asian Education and Development Studies*, 8(4), 443–453.

Clayton, C. H. (2013). Macau's 'Sort-of Sovereignty'. *The Newsletter*, 64, 26–27.

Di Pietro, L., Mugion, R. G., Mattia, G., & Renzi, M. F. (2015). Cultural Heritage and Consumer Behaviour: A Survey on Italian Cultural Visitors. *Journal of Cultural Heritage Management and Sustainable Development*, 5(1), 61–81.

Guangzhou International. (2019). *Guangzhou: The Hub for Intangible Cultural Heritage in the GBA*. Retrieved May 1, 2021, from www.gz.gov.cn/guangzhouinternational/home/citynews/photonews/content/post_3104865.html.

Henderson, J. C. (2008). Conserving Hong Kong's Heritage: The Case of Queen's Pier. *International Journal of Heritage Studies*, 14(6), 540–554.

HKTB. (2021). *Hong Kong Cantonese Opera and Local Cultural Tour*. Retrieved May 1, 2021, from https://partnernet.hktb.com/en/trade_support/tour_planning/explore_hong_kong_tours/hong_kong_cantonese_opera_and_local_cultural_tour/index.html.

ICOMOS. (1998). *ICOMOS Draft Cultural Tourism Charter: Managing Tourism at Places of Heritage Significance*. Melbourne: ICOMOS, Australia International Council on Monuments and Places.

Io, M. U. (2019). Understanding the Core Attractiveness of Performing Arts Heritage to International Tourists. *Tourism Geographies*, 21(4), 687–705.

Luo, J. M., & Lam, C. F. (2016). *Corporate Social Responsibility and Responsible Gambling in Gaming Destinations*. New York, USA: Nova Science Publishers, Incorporated.

Macau Cultural Affairs Bureau. (2016). *The Enchanting Red Boat – An Episode of the Cantonese Operaculture*. Retrieved May 1, 2021, from www.icm.gov.mo/fam/27/en/event.aspx?oldID=2572.

McKercher, B., & Du Cros, H. (2002). *Cultural Tourism: The Partnership Between Tourism and Cultural Heritage Management*. London: Routledge.

McKercher, B., Ho, P. S., & Du Cros, H. (2005). Relationship Between Tourism and Cultural Heritage Management: Evidence from Hong Kong. *Tourism Management*, 26(4), 539–548.

Timothy, D. J., & Boyd, S. W. (2003). *Heritage Tourism*. Harlow: Prentice Hall.

Timothy, D. J., & Boyd, S. W. (2006). Heritage Tourism in the 21st Century: Valued Traditions and New Perspectives. *Journal of Heritage Tourism*, 1(1), 1–16.

UNESCO. (2009). *Yueju Opera*. Retrieved May 1, 2021, from https://ich.unesco.org/en/RL/yueju-opera-00203.

Vong, L. T. N. (2013). An Investigation of the Influence of Heritage Tourism on Local People's Sense of Place: The Macau Youth's Experience. *Journal of Heritage Tourism*, 8(4), 292–302.

Xie, P. F., & Lane, B. (2006). A Life Cycle Model for Aboriginal Arts Performance in Tourism: Perspectives on Authenticity. *Journal of Sustainable Tourism*, 14(6), 545–561.

Yeoh, B. S. (2001). Postcolonial Cities. *Progress in Human Geography*, 25(3), 456–468.

Zhang, J. (2010). *Macau Opera*. Beijing: Culture and Art Publishing House.

Zhang, J. (2017). Intangible Cultural Heritage and Self-Healing Mechanism in Chinese Culture. *Western Folklore*, 197–226.

5 Modernisation and Integration of Cantonese Opera

As a local Chinese opera, Cantonese opera's origin can be traced back to the Qing dynasty. It was popular in Guangdong and Guangxi and later spread to Hong Kong and Macau. Many large and mega troupes, also known as *Sheng gang ban*, performed in many cities, such as Hong Kong and Guangzhou (Lai, 2010). Famous actors or actresses pass along their skills and experiences via the master – apprentice system. In the 1970s, as the number of alternative entertainment forms, such as movies and pop music, increased, Cantonese opera gradually became a minority art form where the elderly are the most common audience. Younger generations lack the motivation to learn and inherit this traditional performing art, causing an inheritance problem.

The inheritance problem roughly began in the 1960s and 1970s, which is also the period when the Chinese experienced the Cultural Revolution. The Cantonese opera community in Hong Kong was also affected. Many local actors and actresses faced difficulty in earning a living, and many of them switched careers. Hence, many troupes did not have enough performers, and the troupes were forced to hire inexperienced performers. This situation caused a decrease in performance quality. At the same time, Cantonese opera schools or training classes stopped teaching traditional Cantonese opera, and the traditional (but professional) training method disappeared. Many graduates from Cantonese opera schools or training classes did not pursue Cantonese opera as their career (Ye, 2008). Whilst successors in schools or training classes are lacking, many famous Cantonese actors or actresses with unique performing styles were ageing. As education became globalised in the 20th century, the training of Cantonese opera performers was restricted by the teaching model adopted from the Western academic world. For example, subjects are classified into different categories, and each subject is taught by academic professionals within a restricted period. However, this teaching mode only provides knowledge and skills. It does not involve practices of social culture, and creativity is not nurtured or

DOI: 10.4324/9781003157564-5

cultivated because these aspects usually require much time and a particular environment to be immersed.

5.1 Modernisation of Cantonese Opera

The modernisation of Cantonese opera usually involves introducing selected Western components into Cantonese opera, the abandonment of some inessential elements in Cantonese opera or the incorporation of Cantonese opera elements into modern musical performance. Regardless of which modernisation type is adopted, all of them face similar questions: Can the resulting products or performance be classified as Cantonese opera, and where does traditional, genuine and authentic Cantonese opera stand? These questions are valid and legitimate, but they are outside the scope of this chapter. However, if the new form of Cantonese opera is executed properly, it should raise the interest of the younger generations, enlighten the passion of the loyal fans and preserve and extend the meaning of aesthetic. Modernisation in Cantonese opera is characterised by cultural incongruities and anachronisms of modern and traditional elements, in the form of mixing the East and the West. It is related to the following issues.

5.1.1 Social Function Fine Art

In 2006, Cantonese opera was enlisted to the first batch of national intangible cultural heritage. The Chinese government has been investing heavily in the development of Cantonese opera, including but not limited to, the construction of cultural environment, preservation and documentation, inheritance and dissemination and teaching apprentices.

After the establishment of the People's Republic of China, Cantonese opera has been developing healthily. The creation of drama is colourful. Inheritance is encouraged, and the genres are developed based on former artists. The artistic charm of both generous singing and shallow singing is enhanced. In addition, the Chinese and Western musicals are combined whilst highlighting the national and local features. Cantonese opera development also includes the introduction of directors to the opera, enhancing the image of the art and developing various designs of the stage art. Given that Cantonese opera is an essential component of the Lingnan culture, one must view this art from the cultural and artistic perspective and should not treat this art as a genre only. According to the vice president of the China Academy of Art and the director of the China Intangible Cultural Heritage Protection Centre, the significance of Cantonese opera goes beyond the opera. It has a unique role in highlighting Lingnan culture.

5.1.2 Infrastructure Boost

The Hong Kong government has been investing heavily in infrastructure to promote Cantonese opera as an intangible cultural resource. For example, the Hong Kong government initiated the Xiqu Centre in 2013. It is an important teaching, learning and performing venue for Cantonese opera located in the West Kowloon District. The Xiqu Centre opened in 2019.

During the opening ceremony of the Xiqu Centre, its chief executive, Carrie Lam, said that Hong Kong has been contributing heavily to Cantonese opera development. In particular, many local community members have been actively developing various ways to preserve this intangible cultural asset and incorporating new elements. 'The innovations of Cantonese opera in Hong Kong in terms of scripts, costumes, music, stage art and performance techniques have made it shine brilliantly', Lam said (West Kowloon Hong Kong, 2019).

In addition to providing a venue for Cantonese opera performances, the Hong Kong government also invites scholars and Cantonese opera participants to teach Cantonese opera to the younger generations. For example, the Xiqu Centre invited Yeung Kim Wah to teach and train young but dedicated artists. Yeung Kim Wah is a famous Cantonese opera actor and director. One of his most famous works is the incorporation and adoption of the Peking Opera, *Farewell My Concubine*, to Cantonese opera. *Farewell My Concubine* is a famous Peking Opera play about Xiang Yu, who is a rival to the Liu Bang and later become the king of the Han dynasty (202 BC to 220 AD).

Guangdong government also invested heavily in Cantonese opera development. For example, the Guangdong Cantonese Opera Protection and Inheritance Regulations was officially announced in 2017. This regulation provides an official state policy guidance towards the support, protection and development of Cantonese opera. It is also one of the largest supports in preserving Cantonese opera as traditional art. In addition, the Guangzhou government formulated the General Work Plan for the Further Revitalization of Cantonese Opera in Guangzhou in 2014 and 2019. The plan involves seven major projects and 15 key tasks. The total amount of investment is more than 800 million renminbi. The projects and tasks include the construction of the Cantonese Opera Art Museum and the relocation of the Guangzhou Cantonese Opera Theatre. The Cantonese Opera Art Museum was built in 2015 with more than 17,000 square meters, and it aims to fill the gap that Guangdong has no professional Cantonese opera museum.

5.1.3 Cultivate Talents: From Apprenticeship to Formal and Non-Formal Education

In December 2018, the Ministry of Education identified the Guangdong Opera Heritage Base of South China University of Technology and the

Guangdong Opera Heritage Base of Xinghai Conservatory of Music as the first batch of excellent traditional Chinese culture heritage bases of national universities. Human resource is the most significant problem that all operas face. When Hung Sin Nui was alive, she mentioned on many occasions that Cantonese opera lacks screenwriters. Cantonese opera is going to be history without good screenwriters. Ensuring a continuous supply of good Cantonese opera is always a problem for the Cantonese opera industry.

The Guangzhou Literature and Art Creation Academe has recently launched the Guangzhou Drama Creation Incubation Plan. This plan hires screenwriters, directors and critics to form an expert panel to nurture and guide creation. The creative teams continue to expand. One of the creative teams, Yangcheng Dram Creation Team, led by Liang Yunan, Li Xinhua, Luo Li, Yu Chuxing, Zeng Zhizhuo, Yang Xiaodan and Wu Hairong, has begun to receive attention. The creative teams also produced many popular Cantonese operas.

According to the chairman of the Guangzhou Cantonese Opera Theatre Co. Ltd., 'Despite there are 23 Plum Blossom Award (which is the Oscar Award for Chinese Opera) winners who are from Guangdong and many young and middle age performers are growing, there should be more development on human resources of Cantonese Opera'. He also said, 'In addition, one should focus more on education. Guangzhou has only one Guangdong Dance and Drama College and there is no Cantonese Opera department in this College. Even when this College recruits a special class related to Cantonese Opera, there are only 30 students. Within these 30 students, there are only less than 50% or, sometimes one-third of the students, who eventually turn professional in Cantonese Opera'. Therefore, he suggested that the Chinese government should provide regular financial support to Cantonese opera development, particularly to the development of Cantonese opera educational programmes in universities or colleges.

Given the support of the government and local community, Cantonese opera education begins to develop in different levels of academic institutions, including kindergarten. In 2015, Xinghai Conservatory of Music established the Xinghai Cantonese Opera Research Society. This society mainly recruits university or college students who are interested in Cantonese opera. Many professional Cantonese opera actors, actresses and workers behind the scenes teach in universities and provide acting and music classes by cooperating with the Guangzhou Cantonese Opera Theatre.

In June 2019, a national first-class actor, Wen Ru Qing, provided an interactive Cantonese opera lecture for acting and singing to more than 500 students in Guangzhou University Affiliated Middle School. Wen said, 'I don't expect Cantonese Opera can root in every child's heart, but I hope that our promotion can make them think Cantonese Opera is fun and beautiful. If that's the case, then that will be great'. Similar activities can also be found in many high schools in Guangzhou.

The party secretary and the dean of the Guangdong Cantonese Opera Theatre said they accumulated many valuable and important Cantonese opera scripts, audios, videos and pictures in the last 60 years. They are now working on digitalising these materials, making a TV show in oral form and recording the ancient Cantonese opera accent. In 2015, Guangdong Cantonese Opera Theatre conducted an experimental trial with Kugou music. They digitalised traditional local operas, such as *Princess Zhaojun*, and Jia Baoyu's *Lament for the Wrong Match in the Arranged Marriage*. Kugou music also created a Cantonese opera subsection and a Cantonese opera tag on their platform. In terms of inheritance protection, Guangdong Cantonese Opera Theatre first established several studios with famous actors or actresses, such that these actors or actresses can demonstrate their skills and talents on stage and teach the young actors and actresses.

According to the party secretary and dean of the Guangdong Cantonese Opera Theatre, Cantonese opera remains popular in the grass root community. According to unofficial statistics, more than 600 Cantonese opera communities exist in Guangdong. Their theatre has performed in many places in Hong Kong, Guangdong and Macau. In 2020, the theatre was booked half a year early. They expected to have more than100 shows in the first two months of next year.

The main difficulty comes with the development in the city and the establishment of a brand name in the city. The young generation and white collars do not know where to watch Cantonese opera even if they are interested. The information is limited. The party secretary and dean believed that the Guangdong Cantonese Opera Theatre has successfully established some brand names, such as Cantonese Opera in the Weekend and The Week of the Famous Actors/Actresses. At first, the attendance was only 20% to 30%. Later, it increased from more than 80% to 90%.

5.1.4 Innovation and Development

The people in the Cantonese opera industry do not usually want to discuss Cantonese opera innovation. One of the reasons is to avoid an argument, particularly with the traditional and famous performers. However, famous Cantonese opera artist, Ding Fan, said otherwise, 'Of course Cantonese Opera is innovating all the time because it has been performing all the time. Shouldn't we innovate to adjust and adapt the market?' Hung Sin Nui also responded to the question 'whether innovation is needed in Cantonese Opera'. She said, 'We are always innovating. Whoever wants to pack and seal Cantonese Opera and avoid it to change does not want Cantonese Opera to exist'.

The Final Battle at Tiance Mansion (hereafter *The Final Battle*), a newly created Cantonese opera by the Guangdong Cantonese Opera Theatre, is a wildly discussed innovation case. This opera was adapted from a 3-dimensional video game, JX3 or *The Fate of Swordsman*. *The Final Battle* is a huge success. In 2015, it won both the National Traditional Opera Box Office and National Newly Created Traditional Opera Box Office issued by Daolue Performing Art Research Centre. Some online comments indicated that viewers began to pay attention to Cantonese opera after watching *The Final Battle*. They would watch any Cantonese opera that they are interested in, regardless of new or traditional repertoire. This development is what the screenwriter of *The Final Battle*, Feng Mingyi, wants to achieve. She said she wants to 'attract some audiences who have never watched or who do not have much understanding of Cantonese Opera'. The director of the Ministry of Culture and Tourism of The People's Republic of China, Xu Haojun, also said, 'this modernisation (of Cantonese Opera) does not show any sense of violation'. *The Final Battle* attracts the younger generation not only because it is an Internet video game but also because it makes Cantonese opera much more fashionable (see Figure 5.1).

Figure 5.1 Younger Generation and Cantonese Opera Video Game

Although Cantonese opera practitioners develop new plays, they also refine the classic plays and perform moderate transformation that fits the aesthetics of the modern audience. For example, the old version of *Searching the Academy*, a classic play that many famous performers presented, was more than 3 hours. The Guangdong Cantonese Opera Theatre compressed the new version to approximately 2 hours. Although some intermediate scenes were deleted, they also increased some group dancing scenes, such as the humorous scene related to the scholar trying to cover up for his friend. The goal is to retain the spirit of Cantonese opera whilst making the audiences think Cantonese opera is fun and interesting, thereby lowering the barriers to engaging Cantonese opera.

5.1.5 Distribution of Cantonese Opera Under the Digital and Internet Generation

When Guangdong Cantonese Opera Theatre presented the modern version of *The Execution Ground of a Wedding* (hereafter, *The Execution Ground*), the play included a kissing scene between the two main characters. This scene was widely discussed. Some critics asked, 'Should we include a daily life scene into the opera stage?' However, Hung Sin Nui said, 'This is amazing. They should kiss each other, mouth to mouth'.

Not long ago, *The Execution Ground* was made into a movie, and the premiere was held in Guangzhou. Hung Sin Niu took many Cantonese opera movies in the last century, such as *Searching the Academy* and *Guan Hanqing*. In her final years, she actively promoted the adaptation of the Cantonese opera *Diao Man Gong Zhu Gan Fu Ma* into a cartoon, and she personally dubbed it.

At present, Guangzhou implements the Guangzhou Cantonese Opera Film Boutique Project. Ten Cantonese opera movies are in line for the next three years, and they will be distributed globally. Amongst these movies, *Nanyue Palace* and *Prince Rui and Princess Zhuang* are expected to arrive soon.

The 8th Yangcheng Cantonese Opera Festival in 2020 concluded successfully in Guangzhou, where 40 highly outstanding performances were presented within nine days. More than 3,000 Cantonese opera industry workers and fans participated and communicated in the festival. In addition, more than 20 Cantonese opera films were played 32 times. The online live broadcast viewers for the newly added Yun Shang Cantonese Opera Festival reached 1.8 billion.

The most eye-catching show in this year's Cantonese Opera Festival selects 21 shows with excellent ideologies, artistic features and appreciative features. Another important show involving overseas Cantonese opera troupes invited troupes from the United States, Canada, New Zealand, Hong Kong, Macau and Guangdong. From these countries, 38 troupes participated. These troupes combined 158 short performances into 21 coherent and connected performances. More than 3,000 artists were involved in the show (Zheng, 2020).

5.2 Integration of Cantonese Opera in the GBA

Guangdong, Hong Kong and Macau are of the same origin. Cantonese opera is the cultural bond that connects the three places. As Cantonese opera has become one of the Intangible Cultural Heritage for 10 years, people from Guangdong, Hong Kong and Macau have joined forces to promote Cantonese opera. Since 2011, the three places have rotated to hold A Showcase of Guangdong, Hong Kong and Macau Cantonese Opera Masters/New Stars every two years, and the shows were extremely popular. The show in 2019 was *Hu Bu Gui*, and all the tickets were sold one month before.

Since 2003, the Yangcheng Cantonese Opera Festival has been the corresponding Oscar for artists from Guangdong, Hong Kong and Macau. Fans can watch six to eight hours of shows a day. The 7th Yangcheng Cantonese Opera Festival attracted more than 200,000 overseas participants. Some people believe that this kind of joint performance or joint festival is helpful to the inheritance of Cantonese opera. Moreover, the three places, Guangdong, Hong Kong and Macau, can learn from one another.

The Cantonese operas in the three places have their own characteristics. In Guangdong, new plays and scripts are created, and the stage performance is very rigorous. In Hong Kong, the plays and the scripts maintain their own tradition, but the stage performance is rather flexible. The Cantonese opera in Macau focuses mainly on group singing concerts. These features are all common consensus of the industry.

From the perspective of Cantonese opera education, the three places communicate frequently. Many Cantonese opera training classes began to recruit with the help of government officials, such as the Department of Culture and Tourism of Guangdong Province, Home Affairs Bureau in Hong Kong and Cultural Affairs Bureau in Macau, and local participants. Some secondary schools began to include Cantonese opera as a part of their teaching programmes or curriculums. The three places continue to hold the Training and Exchange Summer Camp on the Art of Cantonese Opera for the Youth in Guangdong. This summer camp recruits more than 600 students from the primary or secondary schools in the three places to perform certain plays by learning Cantonese opera. Over the years, the students from this summer camp were on a tour of performances in The Southern Theatre in Guangzhou, Ko Shan Theatre in Hong Kong and Cinema Alegria in Macau.

From the communication point of view, students in Hong Kong and Macau can exchange to Guangdong and vice versa to learn from one another. According to Law Kar Ying, a famous Cantonese opera artist in Hong Kong, Cantonese opera can enhance its strengths and reduce weaknesses only when young Cantonese opera participants begin to exchange and learn from one another. It can also be radiated with new vigour and vitality through protection, inheritance and innovation.

According to many experts, Cantonese opera can be learned from one another in the three places or other places in the world because of the common language, Cantonese. According to an old saying, 'Wherever there is Chinese, there is Cantonese Opera'. However, this saying was later modified to 'Wherever there is Cantonese, there is Cantonese Opera'. Hence, people can see how important language is to the distribution and influence of Cantonese opera (Chen, 2019).

Although the three places share a common language, many people are worried that understanding Cantonese opera is challenging. Some said, 'the stage performance is very beautiful, the singing is great, and the plot and genre is understandable, but many people can only follow the subtitles, so they can only enjoy half of the performance'. 'If Cantonese Opera can become "Phantom of the Opera" which is one of the domain opera in the world, then this is the time when Cantonese Opera is raised to the international level and let the world understand Cantonese Opera, as well Chinese culture. We are expecting that day'.

5.3 Summary

The innovation and cooperative development of Cantonese opera are topics of concern to the governments and industry stakeholders in the GBA. When governments adopt relevant measures to support and preserve Cantonese opera, Cantonese opera can be inherited and developed well. Various Cantonese opera stakeholders should keep innovating through social development and keep up with the time to create a unique tourism culture and art in the GBA by fulfilling the needs of modern people for Cantonese opera.

References

Chen, Z. (2019). Young Artists Aim to Preserve Cantonese Opera. *China Daily*. Retrieved June 1, 2021, from www.chinadailyhk.com/articles/137/217/162/1561746725228.html.

Lai, K. (黎鍵). (2010). 香港粵劇敘論 *(Xianggang yueju xulun, Notes on Cantonese Opera)*. Hong Kong: Joint Publishing.

West Kowloon Hong Kong. (2019). Hong Kong's World-Class Performing Arts Venue, the Xiqu Centre, Opens to the Public. *Newsroom*. Retrieved July1, 2021, from West Kowloon Cultural District - Hong Kong's World-Class Performing Arts Venue, the Xiqu Centre, Opens to the Public.

Ye, S. (葉世雄). (2008). *Yiren Weiben, Xinhuo Xiangchuan: Tan Xianggang Yueju Yishu de Baocun he Rencai Peixun. In* 以人為本, 薪火相傳: 談香港粵劇藝術的 保存和人才培訓 *[Be Humane and Carry on the Torch: On Preservation and Talents Training of Cantonese Opera in Hong Kong].* Hong Kong: The International Symposium of Cantonese Opera.

Zheng, H. (郑慧梓). (2020). 第八届羊城粤剧节圆满落幕超1800万人次"云 赏"粤剧节. Retrieved June 1, 2021, from http://news.southcn.com/gd/content/2020-11/26/content_191763238.htm.

6 Residents' Attitudes Towards Cultural Heritage Products

A Case Study of Cantonese Opera in Macau

6.1 Introduction

6.1.1 Importance of Cultural Heritage Tourism

Cultural heritage is rapidly becoming an important resource for tourism worldwide. Cultural heritage, described as an irreplaceable source of life and inspiration, includes monuments, architectural complexes and archaeological sites with outstanding historical, aesthetic, ethnographic or anthropological values (UNESCO, 1972). In addition, cultural heritage tourism refers to experiencing places and activities that truly represent the stories and characters of the past and present (Lussetyowati, 2015). Cultural heritage tourism is one of the most essential and fastest-growing components of the tourism industry and one of the most eye-catching and wide-ranging types of tourism (Richard, 2018; Chen & Wu, 2019). Cultural heritage tourism has recently been recognised by the United Nations World Tourism Organization as an important part of international tourism consumption, accounting for more than 39% of tourists (Richards, 2018).

Cultural heritage is essential because it represents a strong cultural authenticity and promotes a deep understanding of the destination's culture, thereby strengthening the competitiveness of cultural heritage tourism in the broad field of tourism (Gonzalez, 2008), creating social and economic benefits for stakeholders (Esfehani & Albrecht, 2018) and arousing people's awareness of cultural heritage protection (Santa-Cruz, 2016). However, cultural heritage is not a static object but a constantly changing product because of the comprehensive influence of the local economy, social culture and environment (Chang, 1997). Cultural heritage has been easily commercialised into tourist products that satisfy tourists to varying degrees, and the commercialisation process threatens the authenticity of cultural heritage (Kim et al., 2018).

DOI: 10.4324/9781003157564-6

6.1.2 Cultural Heritage Tourism in Macau

Macau has rich cultural heritage assets. Silva (2002) denoted Macau as a 'melting pot of East and West'. Lung (2002) noted that 'Macau has many unique historic buildings and sites, and almost each and every one of them possesses great cultural significance and distinct character'. Macau's tangible heritage resources include 52 monuments, 44 outstanding buildings, 11 sets of buildings and 21 sites scattered around the small city (Ung & Vong, 2010). Amongst these tangible heritage resources, Macau has five famous heritage sites. The five renowned heritage sites are Ruins of St Paul's, Senado Square, A-Ma Temple, Carmel Gardens and Taipa Praia and Taipa Village. These historical places have been propagandised by the local tourist board as must-visit heritage sites (Vong & Ung, 2012). In addition, Macau has precious intangible cultural heritage resources, including Cantonese opera, which is a representative cultural heritage of Macau. Cantonese opera originated in Guangdong Province of China and is regarded as one of Macau's traditional performing arts (Macau Cultural Affairs Bureau, 2016). Similar to other genres of traditional Chinese opera, Cantonese opera combines traditional Cantonese music, singing, string, percussion instruments, martial arts, acting and acrobatics (Io & Chong, 2020). In 2009, Cantonese opera was successfully inscribed on the Representative List of the Intangible Cultural Heritage of Humanity (UNESCO, 2009). All these tributes indicate that Macau has the potential for cultural heritage tourism development.

However, the popularity of Cantonese opera in Macau has gradually declined in recent years, and most local audiences are still elderly residents (Io, 2018). The relevant departments of Cantonese opera have opened some teenager-oriented Cantonese opera classes to train many young Cantonese opera fans and artists; however, the continuous decrease in the number of young Cantonese opera fans challenges the sustainable development of Cantonese opera in Macau (Io, 2018). Therefore, this study investigates the residents' attitudes towards Cantonese opera and tourism development in Macau to increase the popularity of Cantonese opera and promote the sustainable development of Cantonese opera in Macau. This study is divided into five sections. Following this introduction, the second section reviews the literature on residents' attitudes towards cultural heritage tourism and residents' attitudes from a sustainable development perspective. The third section introduces the research methods used in this study. The fourth section analyses and discusses the collected data. The final section summarises the conclusions and implications.

6.2 Literature Review

6.2.1 Residents' Attitudes Towards Cultural Heritage Tourism

Attitude can be defined as an individual state of mind towards a value, which is an enduring psychological tendency that an individual holds towards an object or objects (Getz, 1994). Previous studies on tourism research mainly focused on residents' attitudes towards tourism development (Gursoy et al., 2019). Little research has focused on the residents' attitudes towards heritage tourism. Lee et al. (2007) focused on historical heritage cities in a developed nation and found that the residents' distance from heritage sites, income and place attachment may be the significant factors for their attitudes towards cultural heritage tourism-related issues. Those residents who are locally born, live farther from heritage sites, have a high income and directly depend on tourism are supportive for additional heritage tourism development. Based on social exchange theory and prior studies, Chen and Chen (2010) reveal that the residents' perceptions of the positive and negative impact of heritage tourism and their community attachment have a significant influence on residents' attitudes towards support for heritage tourism. Yuan et al. (2019) found a similar result in an industrial heritage context. Xie et al. (2020) explored the factors influencing residents' attitudes towards heritage tourism development through ground theory approach apart from the quantitative research. The results identified four influential factors: residents' rights, co-creation, community attachment and authenticity.

Most of the studies paid attention to the influential factors and the role of residents' attitudes, and most of them investigated the attitude as an overall concept (Andereck & Vogt, 2000; Chen & Chen, 2010; MacKay & Campbell, 2004; Xie et al., 2020; Yuan et al., 2019). However, the attributes of residents' attitudes did not receive sufficient attention. Heritage includes tangible and intangible objects. The tangible objects refer to historical remnants, whereas the intangible objects refer to cultural assets, such as folk traditions and performing arts. Prior studies of heritage tourism paid much attention to tangible heritage tourism (Lee et al., 2007; Xie et al., 2020; Yuan et al., 2019). Macau, one of the most famous heritage tourist destinations, comprises various element sets and multicultural heritage (Du Cros & Kong, 2020). Andereck and Vogt (2000) revealed that the community has significantly different attitudes towards tourism options. Therefore, heritage tourism in Macau should be investigated in detail. As mentioned, Cantonese opera is one of the cultural heritages in Macau. This case study focuses on the residents' attitudes towards Cantonese opera as a tourism product.

6.2.2 Residents' Attitudes From a Sustainable Development Perspective

Attitude is viewed as a multidimensional construct in previous studies. Attitude measurement has been the focus of several studies. For instance, the residents' attitudes towards the positive and negative impacts of tourism was explored based on social exchange theory (Ribeiro et al., 2017). Moreover, the two-dimensional scale, tourism impact attitude scale (Lankford & Howard, 1994), was widely adopted in previous studies (U. Maruyama et al., 2017). In addition, the measurement scale of residents' attitudes towards economic, sociocultural and environmental impacts of tourism was developed from the sustainability theory perspective (Lundberg, 2017).

Tourism has been widely recognised as one of the most significant economic sectors. The increasing influence of tourism has drawn the attention on sustainable tourism development (Kuščer & Mihalič, 2019). From this perspective, sustainable tourism development has been recognised as a three-dimensional concept referring to economic, sociocultural and environmental sustainability (Streimikiene et al., 2021). Previous studies have explored the attitude towards this three-dimensional sustainability from both positive and negative perspectives.

In a tourism research context, the most influential dimension about the residents' attitudes is the economic dimension (García et al., 2015). On the one hand, the positive impacts on the economic dimension include providing an employment opportunity as an essential income source (Andereck & Nyaupane, 2011), creating a local business environment (Bestard & Nadal, 2007) and improving community infrastructure or public facilities to enhance living standards (Andereck & Nyaupane, 2011). On the other hand, tourism development may also raise the product or service prices, thereby increasing the residents' living costs (Andereck et al., 2005). The effect of tourism on the sociocultural dimension is emphasised on its influence on local customs, social life, beliefs and values (García et al., 2015). On the one hand, the residents may gain opportunities for leisure and cultural activities (Andereck & Vogt, 2000), raise their awareness of preserving heritage resources and enhance their cultural identification (Andereck et al., 2005) through tourism development. On the other hand, various criminal behaviours or vandalism (Diedrich & García-Buades, 2009) was recognised as the negative impacts of tourism on the sociocultural dimension. The environmental dimension mainly focuses on the effect of tourism on local natural resources and the appearance of community surroundings (Andereck & Nyaupane, 2011; Oviedo-Garcia et al., 2008). Previous studies mainly focus on the negative impacts of tourism, including pollution and overcrowding problems (Andereck et al., 2005; McGehee & Andereck, 2004; Yoon et al.,

2001). Sustainable tourism development has become the main paradigm of planning and managing tourism (Kuščer & Mihalič, 2019); thus, the present study adopts this theoretical perspective to explore the residents' attitudes towards Cantonese opera as a tourism resource. The theoretical framework is adopted from previous cultural tourism studies about the residents' attitudes from a sustainable development perspective (see Table 6.1).

Table 6.1 Residents' Attitudes Theoretical Framework

Dimension	Impacts	Salient points	reference
Economic	Positive impacts	Improve income Improve quality of life Attract tourists Reducing seasonality Selling local products Job opportunity Widening economic opportunities Stimulating investment Economic diversification	(Raj et al., 2013; Richards, 2018; Ritchie & Inkari, 2006; Terzidou et al., 2008)
	Negative impacts	Increases price of land and housing Increases price of goods and services Increases local residents' cost of living Competition for land with other economic use Cost for additional infrastructure; jobs may pay low wages Increase imported foreign labour Profits may be exported by foreign investors Increases in road maintenance and transportation systems costs	(Terzidou et al., 2008)
Social-cultural	Positive impacts	Good for local schools Maintaining a rural lifestyle Enjoy visiting local galleries, events and festivals Cultural events give residents an opportunity to meet new people Develop more partnerships to increase the number of cultural events Would like to see more cultural events in my community (such as art festivals) Increase the pride of residents in the community	(Besculides et al., 2002; Ritchie & Inkari, 2006)

Table 6.1 (Continued)

Dimension	Impacts	Salient points	reference
		Community with sufficient information regarding cultural events and festivals	
		Reduced looting and vandalism of cultural historic and religious sites	
		Maintaining town atmosphere	
		Increase commitment to care for resources	
		Stronger community awareness among young	
		Retention of a distinct cultural atmosphere	
		Preservation of cultural heritage	
	Negative impacts	Cultural heritage can be degraded and devalued	(Ritchie & Inkari, 2006)
		Create residents' envy and dissatisfaction	
		Change the socio-economic balance of community	
		Culture becomes divorced from the community residents' everyday lifestyle	
Environment	Positive impacts	Improving physical infrastructure	(Besculides et al., 2002; Raj et al., 2013)
		Increasing residents' environment awareness	
		Maintaining architecture	
	Negative impacts	Traffic and parking problems	(Raj et al., 2013; Ritchie & Inkari, 2006)
		Overcrowding	
		Clashing and unfitting architectural styles	
		Environment erosion	

6.3 Method

This study aims to investigate residents' attitudes towards Cantonese opera and tourism development in Macau. Qualitative methods allow researchers to understand the respondents' subjective opinions, and this method is usually used to determine variables that cannot be adequately described or explained in quantitative research (Strauss & Corbin, 1998). Therefore, the qualitative method of semi-structured interviews was used in this study. Fifteen individual interviews were conducted in May 2021 near the popular Cantonese opera theatre, Estabelecimento De Comidas Tai Long Fong (www.dsedt.gov.mo/lcp/en_US/index.jsp) in Macau. The interviewees were Macau residents. Convenience sampling was first adopted to determine eligible respondents. This study also adopted snowball sampling, and the respondents were asked to invite people from their social networks who met the conditions of this study. A semi-structured interview questionnaire with open-ended questions was adopted to conduct the research. The questionnaire was divided into two parts. The first part aims to collect information about the residents' attitudes towards Cantonese opera and tourism development in Macau, whereas the second part aims to gather demographic information of the interviewees. These questions were formed based on the literature review and were sent to three professional researchers for review.

All interviews were conducted in Chinese. The demographic information of interviewees is presented in Table 6.2. The average duration of each interview was 20 – 40 minutes. All interviews were recorded with the consent of the interviewees and transcribed immediately after each interview was finished. The transcripts were sent to the respondents to ensure accuracy (Mabuza et al., 2014). After verifying the transcript, the corresponding information was entered into NVivo 12.0 for further analysis. Content analysis, which was used to analyse the data of this study, allowed researchers to investigate the text without any influence or directions from any a priori theory or concept; thus, the information revealed from the research is open for discussion (Jennings, 2001). In the initial stage, the three researchers worked on the transcripts separately. The number of interviewees was not predetermined, whilst the researcher continued to conduct interviews until no new information was related to the topic in the interview. A framework was established until consistent results were achieved and no additional information was found from the interviews.

6.4 Results

Relatively strong positive attitudes towards developing Cantonese opera as a tourism product was reflected from the interviewees' data. According to the sustainable development perspective, the residents' attitudes towards this issue is derived from different concerns. The majority of Macau residents paid attention to the sociocultural dimension, such as preserving cultural heritage and retaining a distinct cultural atmosphere. The economic impacts, such as increased destination image and number of attracted tourists, drew the attention of others. A few interviewees also expressed their concerns about environmental impacts, such as maintaining architecture and overcrowding. Table 6.3 presents the summary of attitude attributes and frequency.

Table 6.2 Demographic Information of Interviewees

No.	Gender	Age	Position	Level of education	Living in Macau Years	Last time to get in touch with Cantonese Opera
1	M	18–24	student	Master or Doctor	15	1 month to 1 year
2	M	25–34	work	Bachelor	29	1 month to 1 year
3	M	25–34	work	Master or Doctor	30	1 month to 1 year
4	F	35–44	work	Master or Doctor	39	1 year to 5 years
5	M	45–54	work	Master or Doctor	40	above 5 years
6	F	25–34	work	Bachelor	30	1 year to 5 years
7	F	35–44	work	Master or Doctor	35	above 5 years
8	M	45–54	work	Master or Doctor	40	less than 1 month
9	F	18–24	work	Bachelor	23	1 month to 1 year
10	M	above 65	retired	high school	60	less than 1 month
11	F	above 65	retired	high school	60	less than 1 month
12	F	55–64	retired	high school	50	less than 1 month
13	M	35–44	work	Bachelor	30	1 month to 1 year
14	F	18–24	student	Bachelor	12	1 year to 5 years
15	M	25–34	work	Bachelor	30	1 year to 5 years

6.4.1 Positive Economic Impacts

Various salient points about the positive economic impacts were identified from the interviews based on previous studies of residents' attitudes towards cultural tourism. According to the most frequently concerned item, many residents believed that the unique and traditional elements of Cantonese opera would attract many tourists.

> *Tourists would come and experience with a very novelty Cantonese Traditional Culture through Cantonese opera, which could be very novelty to them and very traditional to Cantonese opera. I believe it is attractive to tourists.*

(I3)

Table 6.3 Macau Residents' Attitudes Towards Cantonese Opera

Dimension	Salient points	Frequency
Economic Positive impacts	Attract tourists	11
	Economic diversification	6
	Improve destination image	4
	Improve income	3
	Improve income by selling products	1
Economic Negative impacts	Decrease or can't improve competitiveness	8
	Job may pay low wages	1
Sociocultural Positive impacts	Community with sufficient information regarding cultural events and festivals	1
	Enjoy visiting local galleries, events and festivals	9
	Give residents an opportunity to meet new people (cultural communication)	4
	Good for local schools	5
	Increase the pride of residents	8
	Preservation of cultural heritage	10
	Promote their local culture	15
	Retention of a distinct cultural atmosphere	13
	Stronger community awareness among young	3
Sociocultural Negative impacts	Culture divorced from the community residents' everyday lifestyle	15
Environment Positive impacts	Maintaining architecture	2
Environment Negative impacts	Overcrowding	2

Many interviewees also believed that developing Cantonese opera as a tourism product could be an effective way to diversify the tourism industry in Macau, given that the major local tourist attraction is gambling (Greenwood & Dwyer, 2017). Given the dominant position of gambling in this area, some residents also believed that developing Cantonese opera may reduce tourists' stereotypes, thereby improving their destination image. The following statements are notable quotes from the interviewees' data.

> *[It] may change Macau's tourism industry, therefore not all products are gambling. At least there is a Cantonese opera. Usually when tourist come to Macau, people said, 'Oh, you're gambling again'. After the development of Cantonese opera, tourists would say, 'I'm going to Macau to watch Cantonese opera'.*

(I1)

Macau's city image would be diversified to change tourists' impression of our city.

(I1)

The possible substantial benefit of developing Cantonese opera was also mentioned by some interviewees. They tended to believe that the new tourist attraction could promote the local tourism industry. In addition, some interviewees expressed that these cultural tourism resources could yield cultural products which would enhance their income. The following statements are notable quotes from the interviewees' data.

The tourists will come. With more tourists, our economy will be better.

(I5)

In fact, I think the handicraft about Cantonese Opera can also be recommended to tourists. Maybe it could perform in some place and then sell this thing.

(I4)

6.4.2 Negative Economic Impacts

Despite the various points of possible positive economic impacts of Cantonese opera development in the local community, some interviewees also expressed their worries on the negative economic impacts. One of the salient points is that Macau could not benefit from the development of this traditional opera to attract tourists because other destinations, such as Guangzhou and Hong Kong, might possess massive markets (e.g., viewers) and resources (e.g., actors). Therefore, these two destinations are more competitive than Macau. Other interviewees also considered that the tourists who come to view Cantonese opera would not induce high consumption. Thus, the job may pay low wages.

Cantonese Opera in Guangzhou despises Cantonese Opera in Macau. Cantonese Opera in Guangzhou is more powerful than that in Macau, so Cantonese people will not come to Macau to watch Cantonese opera.

(I10)

I believe they are not a kind of consumption tourists. We just lack the kind of tourists who stay for a long time or spend a lot of money, right?

(I7)

6.4.3 Positive Sociocultural Impacts

The sociocultural impacts drew major considerations from the interviewees. Various salient points about the positive impacts could be extracted from the interviews. Firstly, many interviewees believed that developing Cantonese opera as a tourism product could provide sufficient information about the related events or festivals for residents. The interviewees also tended to think that some residents would view the developed tourism products as new leisure activities, and these events or festivals would be enjoyed by themselves.

> *Some performances of different Cantonese Opera repertoire stories could let more residents know different repertoire information.*
>
> (I3)

> *Because Cantonese Opera is a very good activity for the elderly. It's very good. It's not a joke, because Cantonese opera can practice Qi. I am also a patient. After listening to Cantonese opera, I feel that I can live to 80 or 90 years old. Because singing Cantonese opera can refine instruments and exercise. I don't like mountain climbing or running. I just sit here and listen to Cantonese opera. I think it's very good. I like the sport of singing Cantonese Opera.*
>
> (I12)

> *I think it would be very convenient to listen to Cantonese Opera in this city, because as its birthplace, it's easy to hear Cantonese opera.*
>
> (I15)

Secondly, the development of this traditional opera was viewed as a kind of leisure activity for residents. Some interviewees also believed that this development could be an effective way for local schools to enhance their community awareness amongst young residents.

> *I think we can do more promotion. Because not many people know where to learn Cantonese opera.*
>
> (I1)

> *If you don't promote it, no one will know it, no one will be interested in learning it, and no one will play it again.*
>
> (I4)

> *Generally, the more things that future generations can learn, the better. We don't want to make the impression of these cultures disappear. This impression is a concept. I don't want future generations not to know whether this thing exists or not. If now intangible cultural heritage is*

gone, and no one mentions this topic now, then future generations will not know. Because future generations don't go back and take the initiative to learn something that has disappeared.

(I2)

Thirdly, the interviewees widely expressed that this development could help the community preserve the local culture, not only the traditional opera itself but also the history, spirit and even language embodied in it. Given that Cantonese opera was a unique heritage in the Cantonese area, some interviewees also considered that tourism development would maintain their community atmosphere, thereby retaining a distinct cultural atmosphere.

And I think that if those things combine the traditional and then the modern, and Cantonese Opera is seen as a representative of China, then I feel more aware of Chinese culture, rather than a place where the west is very western as soon as I come to Macau.

(I14)

Cantonese opera contains many historical stories and heroic deeds. It is very important for Cantonese opera to convey this spirit through performance.

(I1)

Fourthly, the interviewees believed that their Cantonese opera could be promoted to tourists, and their understanding of their culture could increase through tourism development. Other interviewees expressed that this tourism development could enhance their pride in their community.

Because at least we can promote our Cantonese. It's a good way to promote Cantonese. Let more people understand Cantonese through Cantonese opera.

(I1)

There are so many tourists, especially from the mainland or foreign countries. If you promote Cantonese Opera with tourists, you can let more tourists from other provinces and even other countries know what Cantonese Opera is.

(I9)

So, if Macau can attract tourists not only because of the gambling industry, but also because of the Cantonese opera culture, I think it is also a responsibility that Macau should bear. As a resident of Macau, I'm very happy, because after all, it's the government's propaganda, and it can attract more tourists from other places or countries. As a local resident, it must be a very proud thing.

(I9)

Lastly, some interviewees viewed cultural tourism development as an effective way to meet people. The cultural communication brought by this cultural tourism could be a valuable way for them to experience other cultures.

It's important. Macau is an international exchange platform, a platform for China West exchanges, where different cultures converge and cultures are exchanged here.

(I2)

6.4.4 Negative Sociocultural Impacts

Although the traditional Cantonese operas may maintain the community's unique cultural atmosphere and enhance its pride, some interviewees also expressed that Cantonese opera has divorced from their everyday lives. The interview reflected that many residents, particularly young residents, have little knowledge and recognition about this culture. They do not understand this traditional art; therefore, they are not interested in it.

It's the story in Cantonese opera that I don't really understand. There is also their rhythm. The rhythm of activities is relatively slow, which makes me not quite sure what they want to express.

(I13)

First of all, let people like it and understand it. If they don't understand it, they will not be interested in it. Only when they are interested in it, will it spread.

(I7)

Not interested, because it's not popular. Yes. And young people are like the popular direction to cater to the popular, it is not popular.

(I4)

6.4.5 Positive Environmental Impacts

Although Cantonese opera is an intangible cultural resource, some interviewees found its possible role in local theatres. This intangible culture must be exhibited in theatres; thus, much money may be invested in architectural structures. These potential projects can enhance the community appearance and bring positive environmental impacts.

The Macau government would allocate more money to activate theatres.

(I1)

6.4.6 Negative Environmental Impacts

Macau has become one of the most famous tourist destinations in the world. The number of tourists is not its primary concern about tourism development (Lee & Rii, 2016). Given this condition, some interviewees also expressed that developing new tourist attractions and products would induce over-crowding in their community.

I feel that there are too many tourists in Macau. What Macau does not lack is the number of people, that is, the number of tourists.

(I7)

6.5 Conclusions

The sustainable development attitude of residents and their supportive behaviour on tourism development are essential in preserving cultural heritage (Wang, 2016). Previous studies showed that the residents' attitudes towards sustainable tourism development has a positive impact on their community participation and environmentally responsible behaviour, which were identified as essential factors of successful tourism development (Cheng et al., 2019). In the present study, we explored the residents' attitudes towards developing intangible cultural heritage resources as tourism products from the sustainable development perspective. The results revealed various salient points on the economic, sociocultural and environmental aspects.

The salient points of positive and negative economic aspects extracted from this study were consistent with those of the previous cultural tourism studies. On the one hand, the interviewees expressed that developing Cantonese opera as a tourism product could attract many tourists, diversify the local economy, improve destination image, increase their income and sell various products (Raj et al., 2013; Richards, 2018; Ritchie & Inkari, 2006; Terzidou et al., 2008). On the other hand, the wages might not increase through this development. In particular, the lack of competitiveness on cultural resources and markets revealed in this study was not highlighted in the previous cultural tourism studies. Few environmental impacts were also revealed in the present study. On the one hand, exploiting intangible cultural heritage as tourism products may also need tangible settings, such as theatres. Some interviewees believed that Cantonese opera development could promote the investment in local theatres and could maintain the architecture (Besculides et al., 2002; Raj et al., 2013). On the other hand, as a famous tourist destination, Macau may experience overcrowding problems caused by cultural tourism development (Raj et al., 2013; Ritchie & Inkari, 2006). The sociocultural aspects drew most considerations amongst the interviewees and revealed the salient points. The considerations such as providing sufficient information regarding cultural events, enjoying local event visits, helping local schools, increasing the pride of residents, preserving cultural heritage, retaining a distinct cultural atmosphere and promoting strong community awareness amongst the young were consistent with the results of previous cultural tourism studies (Besculides et al., 2002; Ritchie & Inkari, 2006). The promotion of local culture was slightly considered in the existing studies. The intangible cultural tourism embraces the history, spirit and language of a community. Therefore, the development of the intangible cultural heritage as tourism products would deeply promote the community's culture to tourists.

The results mentioned increased our understanding of the residents' attitudes towards culturally sustainable tourism development, and various salient points about Cantonese opera as a tourism product were revealed. The findings of this study could assist the local government and practitioners in developing Cantonese opera. For example, developing Cantonese opera as a tourism product could be an effective way to improve residents' pride, preserve cultural heritage and enhance the community awareness of young generations. Moreover, some possible negative impacts, such as overcrowding and low competitiveness, should be considered when planning the development strategies.

6.6 Limitation and Future Research

Although some contributions were revealed from this study, some limitations and future directions should be considered when explaining the results. Firstly, other interviewees with much diversified demographics, such as different stakeholders, should be included in further studies. Secondly, future studies could adopt quantitative methods to verify the results in this study and develop a measurement scale for residents' attitudes towards developing intangible cultural heritage resources as tourism products. Lastly, residents may have different attitudes towards various cultural heritage products, such as traditional food and festivals. Thus, further studies may investigate the correlation amongst the effect of those products.

References

Andereck, K. L., & Nyaupane, G. P. (2011). Exploring the Nature of Tourism and Quality of Life Perceptions Among Residents. *Journal of Travel Research*, 50(3), 248–260. doi:10.1177/0047287510362918.

Andereck, K. L., & Vogt, C. A. (2000). The Relationship Between Residents' Attitudes Toward Tourism and Tourism Development Options. *Journal of Travel Research*, 39(1), 27–36. doi:10.1177/004728750003900104.

Andereck, K. L., Valentine, K. M., Knopf, R. C., & Vogt, C. A. (2005). Residents' Perceptions of Community Tourism Impacts. *Annals of Tourism Research*, 32(4), 1056–1076. doi:10.1016/j.annals.2005.03.001.

Besculides, A., Lee, M. E., & McCormick, P. J. (2002). Residents' Perceptions of the Cultural Benefits of Tourism. *Annals of Tourism Research*, 29(2), 303–319.

Bestard, A. B., & Nadal, J. R. (2007). Modelling Environmental Attitudes Toward Tourism. *Tourism Management*, 28(3), 688–695. doi:10.1016/j.tourman.2006.04.004.

Chang, T. C. (1997). Heritage as a Tourism Commodity: Traversing the Tourist-Local Divide. *Singapore Journal of Tropical Geography*, 18(1), 46–68.

Chen, C.-F., & Chen, P.-C. (2010). Resident Attitudes Toward Heritage Tourism Development. *Tourism Geographies*, 12(4), 525–545. doi:10.1080/14616688.2010.516398.

Chen, Y. S., & Wu, S. T. (2019). Social Networking Practices of Viennese Coffeehouse Culture and Intangible Heritage Tourism. *Journal of Tourism and Cultural Change*, 17(2), 186–207.

Cheng, T. M., Wu, H. C., Wang, J. T. M., & Wu, M. R. (2019). Community Participation as a Mediating Factor on Residents' Attitudes Towards Sustainable Tourism Development and Their Personal Environmentally Responsible Behaviour. *Current Issues in Tourism*, 22(14), 1764–1782.

Diedrich, A., & García-Buades, E. (2009). Local Perceptions of Tourism as Indicators of Destination Decline. *Tourism Management*, 30(4), 512–521. doi:10.1016/j.tourman.2008.10.009.

Du Cros, H., & Kong, W. H. (2020). Congestion, Popular World Heritage Tourist Attractions and Tourism Stakeholder Responses in Macao. *International Journal of Tourism Cities*, 6(4), 929–951. doi:10.1108/IJTC-07-2019-0111.

Esfehani, M. H., & Albrecht, J. N. (2018). Roles of Intangible Cultural Heritage in Tourism in Natural Protected Areas. *Journal of Heritage Tourism*, 13(1), 15–29.

García, F. A., Vázquez, A. B., & Macías, R. C. (2015). Resident's Attitudes Towards the Impacts of Tourism. *Tourism Management Perspectives*, 13, 33–40. doi:10.1016/j.tmp.2014.11.002.

Getz, D. (1994). Residents' Attitudes Towards Tourism: A Longitudinal Study in Spey Valley, Scotland. *Tourism Management*, 15(4), 247–258. doi:10.1016/0261-5177(94)90041-8.

Gonzalez, M. V. (2008). Intangible Heritage Tourism and Identity. *Tourism Management*, 29, 807–810.

Greenwood, V. A., & Dwyer, L. (2017). Reinventing Macau Tourism: Gambling on Creativity? *Current Issues in Tourism*, 20(6), 580–602.

Gursoy, D., Ouyang, Z., Nunkoo, R., & Wei, W. (2019). Residents' Impact Perceptions of and Attitudes Towards Tourism Development: A Meta-Analysis. *Journal of Hospitality Marketing & Management*, 28(3), 306–333. doi:10.1080/19368623.2018.1516589.

Io, M. U. (2018). Collaboration Between Practitioners and Public Agencies in Preserving and Promoting Musical Heritage in Macau. *Journal of Heritage Tourism*, 1–14.

Io, M. U., & Chong, D. (2020). Determining Residents' Enjoyment of Cantonese Opera as Their Performing Arts Heritage in macao. *Annals of Leisure Research* (3), 1–18.

Jennings, G. (2001). *Tourism Research*. Milton, QLD, Australia: John Wiley and Sons Australia, Ltd.

Kim, S., Whitford, M., & Arcodia, C. (2018). Development of Intangible Cultural Heritage as a Sustainable Tourism Resource: The Intangible Cultural Heritage Practitioners' Perspectives. *Journal of Heritage Tourism*, 1–14.

Kuščer, K., & Mihalič, T. (2019). Residents' Attitudes Towards Overtourism from the Perspective of Tourism Impacts and Cooperation – The Case of Ljubljana. *Sustainability*, 11(6), 1823. doi:10.3390/su11061823.

Lankford, S. V., & Howard, D. R. (1994). Developing a Tourism Impact Attitude Scale. *Annals of Tourism Research*, 21(1), 121–139. doi:10.1016/0160-7383(94)90008-6.

Lee, M. Y., & Rii, H. U. (2016). An Application of the Vicious Circle Schema to the World Heritage Site of Macau. *Journal of Heritage Tourism*, 11(2), 126–142.

Lee, T., Li, J., & Kim, H.-K. (2007). Community Residents' Perceptions and Attitudes Towards Heritage Tourism in a Historic City. *Tourism Hospitality Planning Development*, 4(2), 91–109. doi:10.1080/14790530701554124.

Lundberg, E. (2017). The Importance of Tourism Impacts for Different Local Resident Groups: A Case Study of a Swedish Seaside Destination. *Journal of Destination Marketing & Management*, 6(1), 46–55. doi:10.1016/j.jdmm.2016.02.002.

Lung, D. (2002). The Future of Macao's Past: An Epilogue. *Review of Culture International Edition*, 4, 15–26.

Lussetyowati, T. (2015). Preservation and Conservation Through Cultural Heritage Tourism. Case study: Musi Riverside Palebang. *Procedia-Social and Behavioral Sciences*, 184, 401–406.

Mabuza, L. H., Govender, I., Ogunbanjo, G. A., & Mash, B. (2014). African Primary Care Research: Qualitative Data Analysis and Writing Results. *African Journal of Primary Health Care & Family Medicine*, 6(1), 1–5.

Macau Cultural Affairs Bureau. (2016). *The Enchanting Red Boat-An Episode of the Cantonese Opera Culture*. Macau S.A.R: Cultural Affairs Bureau of the Macau S.A.R.

MacKay, K. J., & Campbell, J. M. (2004). An Examination of Residents' Support for Hunting as a Tourism Product. *Tourism Management*, 25(4), 443–452. doi:10.1016/S0261-5177(03)00127-4.

McGehee, N. G., & Andereck, K. L. (2004). Factors Predicting Rural Residents' Support of Tourism. *Journal of Travel Research*, 43(2), 131–140. doi:10.1177/0047287504268234.

Oviedo-Garcia, M. A., Castellanos-Verdugo, M., & Martin-Ruiz, D. (2008). Gaining Residents' Support for Tourism and Planning. *International Journal of Tourism Research*, 10(2), 95–109. doi:10.1002/jtr.644.

Raj, R., Griffin, K., & Morpeth, N. D. (2013). *Cultural Tourism*. Boston, USA: CABI.

Ribeiro, M. A., Pinto, P., Silva, J. A., & Woosnam, K. M. (2017). Residents' Attitudes and the Adoption of Pro-Tourism Behaviours: The Case of Developing Island Countries. *Tourism Management*, 61, 523–537. doi:10.1016/j.tourman.2017.03.004.

Richards, G. (2018). Cultural Tourism: A Review of Recent Research and Trends. *Journal of Hospitality and Tourism Management*, 36, 12–21.

Ritchie, B. W., & Inkari, M. (2006). Host Community Attitudes Toward Tourism and Cultural Tourism Development: The Case of the Lewes District, Southern England. *International Journal of Tourism Research*, 8(1), 27–44.

Santa-Cruz, T. L. G. F. G. (2016). International Tourism and the UNESCO Category of Intangible Cultural Heritage. *International Journal of Culture, Tourism and Hospitality Research*, 10(3), 310–322.

Silva, R. (2002, September 10–12). Save the Uniqueness of Macao: The Melting Pot of East and West. In Macau Cultural Institute (Ed.), *Proceedings of the Conservation of Urban Heritage: Macau Vision Conference* (pp. 6–25). Macao: Macau Cultural Institute.

Strauss, A., & Corbin, J. (1998). *Basics of Qualitative Research: Procedures and Techniques for Developing Grounded Theory*. Thousand Oaks, CA: Sage.

Streimikiene, D., Svagzdiene, B., Jasinskas, E., & Simanavicius, A. (2021). Sustainable Tourism Development and Competitiveness: The Systematic Literature Review. *Sustainable Development*, 29(1), 259–271. doi:10.1002/sd.2133.

Terzidou, M., Stylidis, D., & Szivas, E. M. (2008). Residents' Perceptions of Religious Tourism and Its Socio-Economic Impacts on the Island of Tinos. *Tourism and Hospitality Planning & Development*, 5(2), 113–129.

U. Maruyama, N., Woosnam, K. M., & Boley, B. B. (2017). Residents' Attitudes Toward Ethnic Neighborhood Tourism (ENT): Perspectives of Ethnicity and Empowerment. *Tourism Geographies*, 19(2), 265–286. doi:10.1080/14616688.2016.1258432.

UNESCO. (1972). *Convention for the Protection of the World Cultural and Natural Heritage*. Paris: UNESCO.

UNESCO. (2009). *Yueju Opera*. Retrieved June 9, 2021, from https://ich.unesco.org/en/RL/yueju-opera-00203.

Ung, A., & Vong, T. N. (2010). Tourist Experience of Heritage Tourism in Macausar, China. *Journal of Heritage Tourism*, 5(2), 157–168.

Vong, T. N., & Ung, A. (2012). Exploring Critical Factors of Macau's Heritage Tourism: What Heritage Tourists Are Looking for When Visiting the City's Iconic Heritage Sites. *Asia Pacific Journal of Tourism Research*, 17(3), 231–245.

Wang, Y. P. (2016). A Study on Kinmen Residents' Perception of Tourism Development and Cultural Heritage Impact. *EURASIA Journal of Mathematics, Science and Technology Education*, 12(12), 2909–2920.

Xie, P. F., Lee, M. Y., & Wong, J. W.-C. (2020). Assessing Community Attitudes Toward Industrial Heritage Tourism Development. *Journal of Tourism Cultural Change*, 18(3), 237–251. doi:10.1080/14766825.2019.1588899.

Yoon, Y., Gursoy, D., & Chen, J. S. (2001). Validating a Tourism Development Theory with Structural Equation Modeling. *Tourism Management*, 22(4), 363–372. doi:10.1016/S0261-5177(00)00062-5.

Yuan, Q., Song, H., Chen, N., & Shang, W. (2019). Roles of Tourism Involvement and Place Attachment in Determining Residents' Attitudes Toward Industrial Heritage Tourism in a Resource-Exhausted City in China. *Sustainability*, 11(19), 5151. doi:10.3390/su11195151.

Index

Printed in the United States
by Baker & Taylor Publisher Services